PRACTICE TESTS FOR THE
TOEFL

Second Edition

TOEFL
TOEFL
TOEFL
TOEFL
TOEFL
TOEFL
TOEFL
TOEFL

Test of English as a Foreign Language

Victor W Mason
Tests and Measurement Office
Kuwait University Language Center

Nelson

Thomas Nelson and Sons Ltd
Nelson House   Mayfield Road
Walton-on-Thames   Surrey
KT12 5PL UK

51 York Place
Edinburgh
EH1 3JD UK

Thomas Nelson (Hong Kong) Ltd
Toppan Building 10/F
22A Westlands Road
Quarry Bay   Hong Kong

© V W Mason 1983, 1989

Original edition first published by
Thomas Nelson and Sons Ltd 1983

This edition first published by
Thomas Nelson and Sons Ltd 1989

ISBN 0-17-555731-4   2nd edition
ISBN 0-17-555448-X   1st edition

NPN 9 8 7 6 5 4 3 2

All Rights Reserved. This publication is protected in the United Kingdom by the Copyright Act 1956 and in other countries by comparable legislation. No part of it may be reproduced or recorded by any means without the permission of the publisher. This prohibition extends (with certain very limited exceptions) to photocopying and similar processes, and written permission to make a copy or copies must therefore be obtained from the publisher in advance. It is advisable to consult the publisher if there is any doubt regarding the legality of any proposed copying.

Printed in Hong Kong

Contents   *page*

Acknowledgements, Preface to the Second
Edition, Dedication   iv, v
Introduction   vi

Practice Test I

Test of Written English	1
Section 1	2
Section 2	10
Section 3	16

Practice Test II

Test of Written English	27
Section 1	28
Section 2	36
Section 3	42

Practice Test III

Test of Written English	53
Section 1	54
Section 2	62
Section 3	68

Practice Test IV

Test of Written English	80
Section 1	81
Section 2	89
Section 3	95

Tapescript   106

Practice Test I	106
Practice Test II	115
Practice Test III	123
Practice Test IV	131

Answer Key   140

Practice Test I	140
Practice Test II	144
Practice Test III	148
Practice Test IV	151

Acknowledgements

Certain listening and reading comprehension passages have been taken or adapted from published articles, as listed below. The cooperation of the following respective sources is gratefully acknowledged:

Listening passages (as transcribed under *tapescript*):
DeWitt Wallace: *In Memoriam* 1889–1981 The Reader's Digest © 1981. Adapted with permission from the Reader's Digest June 1981.
– pages 112–3
Watch Your Weight (But Wisely!) The Harvard Medical School Health Letter December 1980 © 1980 President and Fellows of Harvard College. The Reader's Digest June 1981. – page 130 (bottom)
The Rich and the Poor by Robert Theobald © 1961. – page 139

Reading passages (as found in *Section 3* of each practice test):
Man May Get Rid of Tooth Decay, at Last by Keith Laidler The Guardian © 1980. – page 19 (bottom) and page 73 (top)
Global Warming May Lead to Sea Level Rise Say Scientists The New York Times © 1981. – page 20
A Hugely Deceptive Talent by Sally Holloway The London Press Agency © 1980. – page 21 (bottom)
And Man Created the Chip by Merrill Sheils Newsweek © 1981. All rights reserved. Reprinted by permission. – page 22 (top) and page 46
Calling in Student Loans TIME © 1981. All rights reserved. Reprinted by permission. – pages 23–4
Gold Projected to Rise Substantially The Associated Press – Dow Jones Syndicate © 1981. – page 47 (top)
Robots: Threat to Human Labor Deutsche Presse – Agentur GmbH © 1980. – page 47 (bottom)
A Town is Reborn by Melinda Beck Newsweek © 1981. All rights reserved. Reprinted by permission. – page 48
The Scourage of Senility by Matt Clark Newsweek © 1980. All rights reserved. Reprinted by permission. – pages 50–51
The Humanities Crisis by Kenneth L Woodward Newsweek © 1980. All rights reserved. Reprinted by permission. – pages 73–4
Saying Aloha to Oil by Gerald C Lubenow Newsweek © 1981. All rights reserved. Reprinted by permission. – pages 76–7
Anatomy of a Thunderstorm by Sharon Begley Neweek © 1981. All rights reserved. Reprinted by permission. – page 100 (bottom)
Arctic Ice Cap Preserves Ship for 130 Years by Warren E Leary The Associated Press © 1981. – page 101 (top)
A Meteor Did the Job by Dr John Gribbin The Guardian © 1980.
– page 103 (bottom)
Shaping Life in the Lab by Frederic Golden TIME © 1981. All rights reserved. Reprinted by permission. – page 104

Test of Written English *US Trade 1980–87*. Reprinted with permission from The Economist. – page 80

Every effort has been made to trace holders of copyright. It is hoped that any omission will be pardoned.

Directions to sample questions reprinted by permission of Educational Testing Service. However, the sample test questions were neither provided nor approved by Educational Testing Service.

The material listed above is used in Practice Tests for the TOEFL with the exclusive permission of the respective orginal sources. No part of these listening and reading comprehension passages or test directions may be reprinted without the explicit written authorization of these sources.

Preface to the Second Edition

This new edition of Practice Tests for the TOEFL incorporates some new material and some modifications to the tests in the first edition. Three main changes are involved:

The first is the inclusion of a writing section before each of the four practice tests, in response to the introduction by the TOEFL of the Test of Written English (TWE). A fuller discussion of the TWE, for the benefit of the student, can be found on page viii below.

Also new to the second edition is an expansion of the keys for Section 2, Structure and Written Expression, of each test, to include explanations of the answers.

Finally in the light of further classroom testing of the first edition, it was felt that greater parallelism among the tests could be achieved. Accordingly, some eight of the twenty-eight test parts have undergone changes, including some re-ordering of material. In all four tests, various questions in Section 2, Part B, have been modified. In addition, Section 3, Part A, of Test II has now become Section 3, Part A of Test IV and vice versa. Similarly, Section 1, Part A of Test III and Section 1, Part A of Test IV have changed places – with the corresponding changes in the order of the material on Cassette 2.

Victor W. Mason 1988

Dedication

This book is dedicated to the three persons most responsible for the development of Kuwait University Language Center into a foreign-language teaching institution of stature and distinction: Dr. Yehia El-Ezabi, who as Director from 1976 until 1979 set a standard for administrative excellence recognized by all its staff as worthy of emulation in foreign-language teaching programs anywhere; Dr. Rasha Al-Sabah, Director since 1979, who through times of daunting trial has good-naturedly but firmly striven to keep the Language Center on course in maintaining and raising those standards; and Dr. Donald J. Malcolm, whose tenure as head of the Language Center's Tests and Measurement Office served as a kind of unexpected post-graduate education for those of his testing associates fortunate enough to learn at first hand the vital role that even a small office of measurement and evaluation can play, in attempting constantly to monitor and help raise the academic standards of even a very large university foreign-language teaching program.

Victor W. Mason 1982

Introduction

Format of the TOEFL

Practice Tests for the TOEFL is specifically designed to reproduce the TOEFL format and style as closely as possible, including the instructions, the timing and length of each section, the type of test material, and also the answer sheets. These aspects are vital for you to gain familiarity with the TOEFL.

The TOEFL is divided into three main sections testing five important language skills, either directly or indirectly:

Section	Language Skill	No. of Questions	Time in Minutes
1	Listening Comprehension (3 parts)	50	40
2	Structure and Written Expression (2 parts)	40	25
3	Reading Comprehension and Vocabulary (2 parts)	60	45
Totals	-----	150	110

It will take you about two hours to complete the test, including time for instructions from the test supervisor. It is important for you to note that the three sections are strictly timed, so you must work carefully and steadily in completing each section.

Administration of the TOEFL

Most admissions committees of colleges and universities in the United States, as well as in some other English-speaking countries, require students from foreign countries to submit their TOEFL scores as part of the application process.

The TOEFL is administered in the United States and abroad at officially designated Test Centers. Names and locations of those centers and dates of administration are found in the **Bulletin of Information**, which you may obtain free from Educational Testing Service (ETS) at the following address: TOEFL, Box 899, Princeton, N.J. 08541, U.S.A. The TOEFL **Handbook for Applicants** is also available free of charge from ETS to those who have registered to take the TOEFL.

There is no limit to the number of times you may take the TOEFL. If it is more than two years since you last took the test, your score is no longer regarded as valid, so any new application you make to study at an American college or university must be accompanied by your score from a recent administration of the TOEFL.

The TOEFL Score

Each educational institution in the United States sets its own admissions requirements concerning the English proficiency of applicants whose native language is not English. You may write directly to the college or university of your choice to learn of its particular admission policies. In general, candidates will need to obtain a score above 500 on the TOEFL to be seriously considered for admission to full-time study at most institutions, and above 550 at many of the best-known.

After you have taken the TOEFL, your score will be officially submitted by ETS directly to the institutions you designated to receive it. A copy of the personal score report sent to you will not generally be accepted by those institutions for admission purposes. With your personal score report, you will receive information helping you to interpret your score relative to the performance of a great many other individuals who have taken the test.

ETS, Princeton, uses a statistical procedure to calculate your exact score. The actual score for your test is converted according to a statistical procedure which is described in detail in the *TOEFL Test and Score Manual* available from ETS Princeton. The TOEFL does not have a pass or fail score: an acceptable score depends on the institution to which you apply, and not on the ETS.

Test-Taking Skills

There are certain skills required of you to do well in the TOEFL. A clear knowledge of the style and format of the TOEFL will give you the confidence you need when you take the actual TOEFL. Strictly timed tests like the TOEFL put you under stress, therefore practice in pacing yourself to make effective use of the time allowed will help you avoid panic under pressure. As you do the four practice tests of this book, you should time yourself on each section of each test: in this way, you will know how much time you have for completing and reviewing the questions of each section, and whether you must work more quickly.

The above skills are all related to confidence: beyond that, there is the need to develop your knowledge of English in general. These practice tests are designed to help you with both these aspects of the TOEFL, first when you do the tests, and then when you study your answers in retrospect, using the answer keys and explanatory answers provided at the back of the book.

The Test of Written English

Since the 1986–87 testing year, the TOEFL examination has included a fourth section called the Test of Written English (TWE), administered with the other three sections. The TWE has been introduced in response to the widespread feeling in North American universities that the TOEFL should include a direct measure of student writing ability.

Until now, the TWE has been included with sections 1–3 of the TOEFL only three times a year, administered as the first section of the TOEFL, prior to sections 1–3. After the 30-minute TWE has been given, student writing papers are collected and sections 1–3 are then taken by examinees.

Student writing papers are scored on a six-point scale, with a score of 1 representing a very weak writing sample and a score of 6 indicating virtual native speaker command of the written language. The TWE score is reported separately from the TOEFL score calculated on the basis of sections 1–3.

Every TWE writing topic will be a task asking the student either 1) to compare and/or contrast two opposing points of view and to support one of those positions; or 2) to describe and interpret a chart or graph. In each case, examinees are expected to respond to all parts of the writing question, to organize their thoughts carefully, to write clearly in answering the questions, and to support their positions with examples, data, or other relevant evidence.

With the sample questions in this book, examinees should use extra sheets of paper to 1) make a short list of their main ideas, in no particular order; 2) rearrange those ideas into a logical outline; and 3) write a rough first draft concentrating on including all important ideas. They should not worry too much in the first draft about mechanics like spelling and minor punctuation points. Polishing the language and attention to mechanical detail should be done in the final draft.

Examinees should spend about one fourth of their time (not more) on preparation, about one half of the time in writing the first draft, and the remaining time on writing the final draft.

Practice Test I

Test of Written English

Time: 30 minutes

Some people think that the richer countries have a responsibility to help the poorer ones. Other people claim that such 'help' often causes more problems than it solves. Compare these two conflicting claims and explain which you think is the better policy.

You may make notes.

Practice Test I

Section 1
Listening Comprehension

Time: 40 minutes

In this section of the test, you will have an opportunity to demonstrate your ability to understand spoken English. There are three parts to this section, with special directions for each part.

Part A

Directions: For each problem in Part A, you will hear a short statement. The statements will be spoken just one time. They will not be written out for you, and you must listen carefully in order to understand what the speaker says.

When you hear a statement, read the four sentences in your test book and decide which one is closest in meaning to the statement you have heard. Then, on your answer sheet, find the number of the problem and mark your answer.

Listen to the following example:

You will hear:
You will read: (A) Anne doesn't like her brother.
(B) Anne usually eats no breakfast.
(C) Anne eats a smaller breakfast than her brother.
(D) Anne's brother eats as much as she does for breakfast.

Sample Answer
Ⓐ Ⓑ ● Ⓓ

Sentence (C), "Anne eats a smaller breakfast than her brother," means most nearly the same as the statement: "Unlike her brother, Anne usually prefers a small breakfast." Therefore, you should choose answer (C).

Listen to the next example:

You will hear:
You will read: (A) Mrs. Weller owns a lot of expensive jewelry.

Sample Answer
Ⓐ ● Ⓒ Ⓓ

(B) Mrs. Weller is wearing a lot of expensive jewelry today.
(C) Mrs. Weller is lucky to be married to such a wealthy man.
(D) Mrs. Weller's family owns the biggest jewelry store in town.

Sentence (B), "Mrs. Weller is wearing a lot of expensive jewelry today," is closest in meaning to the sentence: "Mrs. Weller has on a fortune in jewelry." Therefore, you should choose answer (B). Now continue.

1. (A) Someone helped the conductor to his feet.
   (B) The audience clapped loudly for the musicians.
   (C) Someone presented the orchestra a beautiful bouquet of flowers.
   (D) The audience noisily demonstrated its disappointment with the concert.

2. (A) Marvin had to work and couldn't attend college.
   (B) Marvin began college but had to drop out to get a job.
   (C) Marvin paid for his college education by working at the same time.
   (D) With a bank loan, Marvin didn't have to work while studying at college.

3. (A) Janet forgot her purse and her license.
   (B) Janet forgot her license but not her purse.
   (C) Janet forgot her purse but not her license.
   (D) Janet forgot neither her license nor her purse.

4. (A) Laura's parents told her to turn on the TV.
   (B) Laura noticed her parents watching TV.
   (C) Laura's parents found her watching TV.
   (D) The TV was on a table in Laura's room.

5. (A) The shopping center has a lot of parking places.
   (B) There are very few problems at the city park.
   (C) The city park is near the shopping center.
   (D) The park and the shopping center have very few problems.

6. (A) Jack didn't listen to other people's opinions.
   (B) Jack's views were generally considered strange.
   (C) Jack had very few opinions of his own.
   (D) Jack didn't let others' views affect his own.

7. (A) Honestly, cigarettes make me ill.
   (B) Frankly, the taste of cigarettes doesn't bother me.

Listening Comprehension

    (C) In fact, I strongly dislike the taste of cigarettes.
    (D) As a matter of fact, I prefer to be seated while smoking.

8 (A) Tom saw how to treat his cattle.
   (B) The vet came to inspect Tom's cattle regularly.
   (C) Tom wanted to find out his animals' problem.
   (D) Tom and the vet watched his cattle feeding.

9 (A) Bill generally falls into a deep sleep.
   (B) Bill snores loudly while sleeping.
   (C) Bill frequently talks in his sleep.
   (D) Bill often walks in his sleep at night.

10 (A) Mrs. Carson wanted her daughters to be more polite while eating.
    (B) Mrs. Carson wanted her daughters to leave the dinner table.
    (C) Mrs. Carson wanted her daughters to eat a little more slowly.
    (D) Mrs. Carson wanted her daughters to remember all meal times.

11 (A) Carol told Jeff she couldn't solve the math problem.
    (B) It seemed that Carol was angry at Jeff.
    (C) Carol had nothing to say to Jeff.
    (D) It wasn't clear to Jeff what Carol's problem was.

12 (A) The Landons decided to go to see the basketball game.
    (B) The Landons argued about going to see the basketball game.
    (C) The Landons refused to consider going to see the basketball game.
    (D) The Landons thought it was too far to go to see the basketball game.

13 (A) The driver does not give the passengers any tickets.
    (B) Passengers can not use cash and must pay for their tickets by check.
    (C) Passengers deposit the exact fare and receive a ticket in return.
    (D) Passengers hand the driver their fare and take a ticket from a box.

14 (A) Margaret decided to go to Paris since she did not have to pay herself.
    (B) Margaret decided not to go to Paris and got her money back.
    (C) Margaret was undecided about going to Paris but bought a ticket anyway.
    (D) Margaret could not make up her mind about going to Paris until it was too late to go.

15 (A) The editor was jealous of Ted's abilities.
    (B) The editor promoted Ted for a job well done.
    (C) Ted was dissatisfied with his job and left.
    (D) Ted lost his job because of sloppy work.

Practice Test 1

16. (A) Just pay the bill and let's go.
    (B) Give the waiter a 10 per cent tip but no more.
    (C) With a service charge, the waiter should not expect a tip.
    (D) The restaurant should not charge more than a 10 per cent service charge for such a meal.

17. (A) Mrs. Douglas left the shop counting her money.
    (B) Mrs. Douglas accidentally forgot a package at the shop.
    (C) Mrs. Douglas decided not to buy anything after all.
    (D) Mrs. Douglas thought the clerk was not telling the truth.

18. (A) It's a quite pleasant day outside.
    (B) It's nice outside but Betty doesn't want to go anywhere.
    (C) It's so warm outside that it's better to stay cool inside.
    (D) On such a cold day, it's nice to be comfortable in a warm home.

19. (A) The tickets have just gone on sale.
    (B) All the tickets have been sold.
    (C) The concert has been canceled.
    (D) The lady still has a few tickets for sale.

20. (A) Mr. and Mrs. Collins are living in separate homes.
    (B) Mr. Collins is away from home on business now.
    (C) Mrs. Collins said she is waiting for her husband to return from a business trip.
    (D) Mr. and Mrs. Collins became separated in the large crowd.

Part B

Directions: In Part B you will hear fifteen short conversations between two speakers. At the end of each conversation, a third voice will ask a question about what was said. The question will be spoken just one time. After you hear a conversation and the question about it, read the four possible answers and decide which one would be the best answer to the question you have heard. Then, on your answer sheet, find the number of the problem and mark your answer.

Listen to the following example:

You will hear:

You will read: (A) A month.
              (B) 1½ months.
              (C) Two months.
              (D) 2½ months.

Sample Answer

(A) (B) (C) ●

From the conversation, we know that the friends will leave in mid-June and return in late August. The best answer, then, is (D), "2½ months." So you should choose answer (D). Now continue.

Listening Comprehension

21. (A) His car was hit by another car.
    (B) He was hurt while involved in sports.
    (C) He fell down some stairs.
    (D) While crossing a street, he was hit by a car.

22. (A) To a play.
    (B) To a movie.
    (C) To a concert.
    (D) To a night club.

23. (A) Attending the party.
    (B) Visiting some friends.
    (C) Studying for an exam.
    (D) Getting over an illness.

24. (A) By phoning a special number.
    (B) By looking at the bulletin boards.
    (C) By attending social events regularly.
    (D) By reading the campus newspaper.

25. (A) By express mail.
    (B) Via air mail.
    (C) By registered mail.
    (D) Via air mail express.

26. (A) Confident that it works.
    (B) Skeptical that it helps.
    (C) Optimistic about eventual cures.
    (D) Pessimistic about modern medicine.

27. (A) He uses a newer machine.
    (B) His union went on strike.
    (C) His job is now done by a machine.
    (D) His job was given to another worker.

28. (A) She has just died.
    (B) She went home after church.
    (C) She has not felt well lately.
    (D) She will attend church tomorrow.

29. (A) It comes by mail.
    (B) It arrives earlier than at the newsstand.
    (C) Going to the newsstand is inconvenient.
    (D) It's much cheaper than at the newsstand.

30. (A) Too hard-working.
    (B) Very dependable.
    (C) Rather boastful.
    (D) Strong in mathematics.

31. (A) One traffic ticket.
    (B) Two traffic tickets.
    (C) A warning not to speed again.
    (D) A scolding for forgetting his license.

32. (A) He bought it second-hand.
    (B) He bought it new.
    (C) He bought it on installments.
    (D) He needed a bank loan to buy it.

33 (A) Excited.
(B) Pleased.
(C) Frightened.
(D) Disappointed.

34 (A) That it's too expensive.
(B) That it isn't needed.
(C) That it should be built.
(D) That a college would be better.

35 (A) Only English.
(B) Only the foreign language.
(C) Mostly the students' language.
(D) Each language about half the time.

Part C

Directions: In this part of the test, you will hear several short talks and/or conversations. After each talk or conversation, you will be asked some questions. The talks and questions will be said just one time. They will not be written out for you, so you will have to listen carefully in order to understand and remember what the speaker says.

When you hear a question, read the four possible answers in your test book and decide which one would be the best answer to the question you have heard. Then, on your answer sheet, find the number of the problem and fill in (blacken) the space that corresponds to the letter of the answer you have chosen.

Listen to this sample talk:

Now listen to the first question on the sample talk:

You will hear:

Sample Answer

Ⓐ ● Ⓒ Ⓓ

You will read: (A) Those emphasizing the profit motive.
(B) Those reflecting social values he admired.
(C) Those promoting his religious views.
(D) Those written by the best fiction writers.

The best answer to the question, "What kind of articles did Mr. Wallace mainly select for his magazine?" is (B), "Those reflecting social values he admired." Therefore, you should choose answer (B).

Now listen to the second question on the sample talk:

You will hear:

Sample Answer

Ⓐ Ⓑ ● Ⓓ

You will read: (A) To stress the magazine's lack of seriousness.
(B) To teach readers many new jokes.

Listening Comprehension

        (C) To indicate Mr. Wallace's love of life.
        (D) To show that non-fiction is funnier than fiction.

The best answer to the question, "What is the speaker's probable purpose in mentioning humor in the *Digest*?" is (C), "To indicate Mr. Wallace's love of life." Therefore, you should choose answer (C). Now continue.

36 (A) Good.   (C) Almost new.
    (B) Fair.   (D) Excellent.

37 (A) He doesn't like it.   (C) It's no longer attractive.
    (B) He's going overseas.   (D) It's too expensive for him.

38 (A) The price of the car.   (C) The age of the car.
    (B) The man's address.   (D) The man's reason for leaving.

39 (A) In three days.   (C) The following week.
    (B) The same evening.   (D) The following morning.

40 (A) They have a reservation.
    (B) The motel has several vacancies.
    (C) They are friends of the owner.
    (D) Someone else canceled a reservation.

41 (A) A color television.   (C) An extra bedroom.
    (B) A swimming pool.   (D) A second-floor unit.

42 (A) Prior to arrival.   (C) When they reserve a room.
    (B) While they register.   (D) Just before their departure.

43 (A) Some guests may not be honest.
    (B) The policy is required by law.
    (C) No. 61 is a luxury unit.
    (D) The owners are simply greedy.

44 (A) The plane is going to land.
    (B) The plane is going to take off.
    (C) The air might become very rough.
    (D) So children won't run around.

45 (A) Order drinks.   (C) Attempt to sleep.
    (B) Smoke cigarettes.   (D) Use the lavatories.

46 (A) When a steward says so.
    (B) When the seat-belt sign goes off.
    (C) When they become hungry.
    (D) When the captain makes another announcement.

47 (A) To represent his firm.
   (B) To have an interview.
   (C) To pay a social call.
   (D) To service a computer.

48 (A) As a valuable employee.
   (B) As an average employee.
   (C) As an unqualified employee.
   (D) As a troublesome employee.

49 (A) Surprised.
   (B) Uncertain.
   (C) Bored.
   (D) Hopeful.

50 (A) An employee's age.
   (B) An employee's loyalty.
   (C) An employee's ability.
   (D) An employee's length of service.

THIS IS THE END OF THE LISTENING COMPREHENSION PORTION OF THE TEST. LOOK AT THE TIME NOW, BEFORE YOU BEGIN WORK ON SECTION 2. USE *EXACTLY 25 MINUTES* TO WORK ON SECTION 2.

Section 2
Structure and Written Expression

Time: 25 minutes

This section is designed to measure your ability to recognize language that is appropriate for standard written English. There are two types of questions in this section, with special directions for each type.

Part A

Directions: In Part A each problem consists of an incomplete sentence. Four words or phrases, marked (A), (B), (C), (D), are given beneath each sentence. You are to choose the one word or phrase that best completes the sentence. Then, on your answer sheet, find the number of the problem and mark your answer.

Example I.

We got a lot of exercise during our holiday in the Swiss Alps ----- skiing every day.

(A) to   (C) in
(B) by   (D) on

Sample Answer
Ⓐ ● Ⓒ Ⓓ

In English, the sentence should read, "We got a lot of exercise during our holiday in the Swiss Alps by skiing every day." Therefore, you should choose (B).

Example II.

Los Angeles never gets snowstorms and Honolulu -----.

(A) is too.   (C) isn't either.
(B) does too.   (D) doesn't either.

Sample Answer
Ⓐ Ⓑ Ⓒ ●

The sentence should read, "Los Angeles never gets snowstorms and Honolulu doesn't either." Therefore, you should choose (D).

As soon as you understand the directions, begin work on the problems.

1. While formerly a member of the sports club, Mr. Teeters ----- tennis there regularly.

   (A) is used to playing   (C) used to play
   (B) was used to play   (D) used to playing

Practice Test I

2 Some scientists say it is essential that mankind ----- the amount of air pollution in big cities.

   (A) reduce
   (B) reduced
   (C) be reduced
   (D) will reduce

3 Having arrived at the football stadium barely in time, -----.

   (A) the two teams were just starting as we sat down.
   (B) we reached our seats just as the game started.
   (C) the officials had already blown the whistle for the game to start.
   (D) the gatekeeper took our tickets as we passed.

4 ----- the rhinoceros is carefully protected, it will soon go the way of other extinct species.

   (A) If
   (B) Therefore
   (C) As long as
   (D) Unless

5 Most of the courses at the banquet were completely consumed, but there ----- food still remaining.

   (A) were few
   (B) was little
   (C) were a few
   (D) was a little

6 A person probably picks up any language most easily ----- it as a child outside a classroom.

   (A) learn
   (B) to learn
   (C) by learning
   (D) for learning

7 The boys' father built them a large sandbox -----.

   (A) to play in
   (B) to play in it
   (C) to play in there
   (D) in which to play in there

8 This beach is usually closed ----- a rainy day.

   (A) in
   (B) on
   (C) at
   (D) while

9 The movie was very boring and many people began to leave early. By the end, most people -----.

   (A) had already left
   (B) were already leaving
   (C) were already left
   (D) had already been leaving

10 The little boy first took off one shoe and then took off -----.

   (A) other
   (B) another
   (C) the other
   (D) each other

Structure and Written Expression

11 That's not the butcher we always buy our meat from; you've gone to ------ one.

   (A) wrong
   (B) a wrong
   (C) the wrong
   (D) some wrong

12 After years of great unhappiness in her life, Mrs. Palmer one day just seemed to go -----.

   (A) mad
   (B) madly
   (C) madder
   (D) madness

13 The police are accusing this businessman of having his store ----- up so that he could collect the insurance.

   (A) blow
   (B) blown
   (C) blew
   (D) blowing

14 Hardly ever ----- get a good job these days without a good education.

   (A) people might
   (B) do people
   (C) people can
   (D) have people

15 The Joneses' corn did very well this year, so at harvest time they gave us quite -----.

   (A) many of them
   (B) a few of them
   (C) much of it
   (D) a lot of it

Part B

Directions: In questions 16–40 each sentence has four words or phrases underlined. The four underlined parts of the sentence are marked (A), (B), (C), (D). You are to identify the one underlined word or phrase that should be corrected or rewritten. Then, on your answer sheet, find the number of the problem and mark your answer.

Example I.   Sample Answer

   One of Mrs. Wilson's <u>daughters</u> <u>doesn't</u> play   Ⓐ Ⓑ ● Ⓓ
                            A   B
the piano as <u>skillful</u> as the other one <u>does</u>.
                C   D

Answer (C), the underlined adjective skillful, would not be accepted in carefully written English. The adverb skillfully should be used instead. Therefore, the sentence should read: "One of Mrs. Wilson's daughters doesn't play the piano as skillfully as the other one does." To answer the problem correctly, you would choose (C).

Example II.   Sample Answer

   The woman <u>said</u> she <u>had saw</u> the robbery   Ⓐ ● Ⓒ Ⓓ
                  A   B

take place on the previous day.
    C   D

Answer (B), the underlined phrase had saw, should not be used in carefully written English. The form seen should be used after had. Therefore, the sentence should read, "The woman said she had seen the robbery take place on the previous day." To answer the problem correctly, you would choose (B).

As soon as you understand the directions, begin work on the problems.

16 Nelson could of won the fight, with a little more training and a better
           A   B   C   D
manager.

17 The cost of fruits and vegetables go up and down partly because of
             A   B   C   D
seasonal factors.

18 Professor Watford asked his students to explain himself more clearly
                 A   B   C
than they had so far done.
       D

19 It was on the second days of our camping trip that the storm suddenly
                 A   B   C
struck and destroyed much of our equipment.
  D

20 While in Los Angeles, visitors have the chance to do many interesting
    A   B
things, such as attending concerts and seen Hollywood and Disneyland.
        C   D

21 Pedestrians should across this wide boulevard only when they have the
         A   B   C   D
green light.

22 Between Mt. Everest and Mt. Kilimanjaro, the former is the highest.
    A   B   C   D

23 At the busiest airports, flights are often delayed as result of
       A   B   C
very heavy traffic.
  D

24 The policeman found out the burglar hiding in the basement of the
                          A   B
jewelry shop while the alarm was still ringing.
    C   D

Structure and Written Expression

25 It is commonly understand that one kilogram is equal to about
    A   B   C   D
    2.2 pounds.

26 Yugoslavia has been one nation for many years, even though it is
                                    A   B
    composed by people of several different nationalities, languages and
             C   D
    religions.

27 In sport, as in war, the side with the greater strength usually win.
    A   B   C   D

28 Lack of a certain chemical in the blood of some people makes it is
    A   B   C
    impossible for bleeding to stop in the event of an injury.
                                              D

29 When a country's currency is devalued, imports from abroad then
    A   B   C
    more cost.
    D

30 In recent years, the best-known Japanese firms have managed to
       A   B   C
    outperform those of the majority of their foreign competitors.
               D

31 Heart attacks and strokes can be caused by clots that block arteries and
    A   B
    resulting in great damage to the heart or brain.
    C   D

32 The World War I began in 1914 after Archduke Ferdinand of Austria–
    A   B   C
    Hungary had been assassinated.
            D

33 Antarctica has so cold temperatures that no one is able to live there
                  A   B   C
    permanently.
    D

34 Human health and the environment must be protected, but many
                    A   B
    countries emphasize more the need to economic development.
                                     C   D

Practice Test I

35 The decision to raise or lower the world price of oil is very up to OPEC; it
                                  A   B   C
is really not for other countries to make.
            D

36 The theory behind foreign aid is that the richer countries have an
              A   B   C
obligation to do something to the poorer ones.
            D

37 American universities have been cutting their costs by reducing the
             A   C   C
percentage of full-time teaching positions and increasing the part-time
one.
D

38 Mrs. Carter and Mrs. Reagan they became well-known for their efforts
          A   B
to deal with serious social problems.
  C   D

39 The child received many lovely gifts on her birthday, probably more than
            A   B
it was good for her.
C   D

40 Mrs. Lincoln was sitting besides the President when he was shot at Ford's
         A   B   C D
Theater in Washington in 1865.

DO NOT WORK ON ANY OTHER SECTION OF THE TEST.

IF YOU FINISH IN LESS THAN 25 MINUTES,
CHECK YOUR WORK ON SECTION 2 ONLY. AT THE
END OF 25 MINUTES, GO ON TO SECTION 3.
USE *EXACTLY 45 MINUTES* TO WORK ON SECTION 3.

Section 3
Reading Comprehension and Vocabulary

Time: 45 minutes

There are two types of questions in this section, with special directions for each type.

Part A

Directions: In questions 1–30 each sentence has a word or phrase underlined. Below each sentence are four other words or phrases. You are to choose the one word or phrase which would best keep the meaning of the original sentence if it were substituted for the underlined word or phrase. Look at the example.

Example.   Sample Answer

The lecture hall is practically full now.   Ⓐ Ⓑ ● Ⓓ

(A) half   (C) almost
(B) hardly   (D) completely

The best answer is (C), because the sentence, "The lecture hall is almost full now," is closest in meaning to the original sentence, "The lecture hall is practically full now." Therefore, you should mark answer (C).

As soon as you understand the directions, begin work on the problems.

1 We encountered the Smiths before leaving the parking lot.

   (A) met   (C) helped
   (B) saw   (D) surprised

2 Mr. Edwards is always very candid in his discussions.

   (A) frank   (C) pleasant
   (B) alert   (D) agreeable

3 We occasionally see John here in town.

   (A) often   (C) seldom
   (B) never   (D) sometimes

4 The fundamental reason for his illness has never been discovered.

   (A) basic   (C) obvious
   (B) severe   (D) physical

5 My wife has been asked to write an article for the newspaper about the consequences of alcohol consumption.

   (A) profits
   (B) results
   (C) dangers
   (D) pleasures

6 The government has licensed this company to produce weapons.

   (A) suddenly hired
   (B) recently founded
   (C) legally permitted
   (D) secretly purchased

7 The President forecast that war would soon break out between the two neighboring states.

   (A) hinted
   (B) worried
   (C) predicted
   (D) disagreed

8 Today's class has already been called off.

   (A) revised
   (B) canceled
   (C) completed
   (D) announced

9 The prisoners were liberated as soon as the new government took over.

   (A) told
   (B) freed
   (C) moved
   (D) aided

10 When did Miss Perkins pass away?

   (A) die
   (B) marry
   (C) leave
   (D) decide

11 Contrary to popular belief, this snake is quite innocuous.

   (A) rare
   (B) common
   (C) harmless
   (D) dangerous

12 These brown insects are ubiquitous, aren't they?

   (A) eaten by birds
   (B) found everywhere
   (C) very destructive
   (D) useful to farmers

13 Our friends said they were beginning their studies of Russian in earnest next semester.

   (A) eagerly
   (B) seriously
   (C) as a hobby
   (D) for a degree

14 Employees were told to take their grievances to the assistant manager.

   (A) salaries
   (B) customers
   (C) complaints
   (D) suggestions

Reading Comprehension and Vocabulary

15 Her son is a veterinarian.

   (A) a war veteran
   (B) an expert cook
   (C) a famous actor
   (D) an animal doctor

16 The Carsons were optimistic that their son would be able to leave the hospital for Christmas.

   (A) hopeful
   (B) certain
   (C) doubtful
   (D) surprised

17 As soon as you are sure, try to get in touch with me, would you please?

   (A) assist me
   (B) contact me
   (C) hold my hand
   (D) go to my house

18 It is unwise to provoke strange animals.

   (A) feed
   (B) touch
   (C) anger
   (D) chase

19 Robert was regarded as a profound thinker by his friends.

   (A) a deep
   (B) a lazy
   (C) a careful
   (D) an original

20 These housing projects must be designed and built according to very strict criteria.

   (A) locations
   (B) relations
   (C) contracts
   (D) standards

21 No one could recall when that event had taken place.

   (A) begun
   (B) occurred
   (C) been reported
   (D) been completed

22 Tom alluded to Mary at one point in the play.

   (A) spoke with
   (B) explained to
   (C) met with
   (D) referred to

23 They say he and his brother are gullible, you know.

   (A) very unpopular
   (B) easily deceived
   (C) physically similar
   (D) generally frustrated

24 Don't argue with me – *I'm* treating this time!

   (A) paying
   (B) complaining
   (C) going to phone
   (D) planning to leave

Practice Test I

25 When equipment becomes obsolete, it is time to replace it.

   (A) run down   (C) badly rusted
   (B) out of date   (D) expensive to repair

26 Jane receives low marks from her teacher every once in a while.

   (A) very seldom   (C) rather frequently
   (B) all the time   (D) from time to time

27 I am glad to hear about the young man's good convalescence.

   (A) recovery   (C) appearance
   (B) response   (D) appointment

28 The statement was attributed to Dr. Kohler.

   (A) angrily denied by   (C) presumably repeated by
   (B) reportedly said by   (D) carelessly published by

29 Few boxers have been as outstanding as the present heavyweight champion.

   (A) powerful   (C) excellent
   (B) handsome   (D) talkative

30 Weren't those two writers contemporaries?

   (A) equally famous   (C) familiar with each other
   (B) hostile to each other   (D) living at the same time

Part B

Directions: The remaining questions in this section are based on a variety of reading material (single sentences, paragraphs, advertisements, and the like). In questions 31–60, you are to choose the one best answer, (A), (B), (C), or (D), to each question. Then on your answer sheet, find the number of the problem and mark your answer. Answer all questions following a passage on the basis of what is stated or implied in that passage.

   Read the following sample passage.
   Normally, the human body combats an infection by producing antibodies to the invading disease. These seek out the intruder and destroy it. These antibodies persist in the bloodstream for long periods and prevent reinfection.

Example I.   Sample Answer

   The passage says that the main function of
   antibodies is to

19

Reading Comprehension and Vocabulary

   (A) attack the human body.
   (B) invade other organisms.
   (C) produce other antibodies.
   (D) fight invading diseases.

The passage says that the body fights (combats) disease by producing antibodies. Therefore, you should choose answer (D).

Example II: Sample Answer

The article says that, after an infection from
a particular disease has been cured, the
antibodies

   (A) all disappear.
   (B) continue to increase.
   (C) remain in the blood.
   (D) gradually decline in number.

The passage says that the antibodies remain (persist) in the blood for a long time and prevent the disease from recurring. Therefore, you should choose (C) as the best completion of the sentence. Now continue.

Questions 31–35

Carbon dioxide in the atmosphere, which is primarily a result of mankind's burning of fuels, is thought to act like the glass of a greenhouse. It absorbs heat radiation from the earth and its atmosphere, heat that otherwise would dissipate into space.

The possibility that the greenhouse effect could alter the earth's temperature has been debated for many years. Scientists have agreed that carbon dioxide is increasing but there has been uncertainty about whether temperatures are also increasing. The major difficulty in accepting the greenhouse effect has been the absence of observed warming coincident with the historic carbon dioxide increase.

31 The principal consequence of the greenhouse effect is assumed to be an increase in

   (A) global temperatures.
   (B) the building of greenhouses.
   (C) the burning of fossil fuels.
   (D) the sun's radiation reaching earth.

32 The carbon dioxide in the atmosphere is believed to produce the greenhouse effect by

   (A) being burned on the ground.
   (B) dissipating into outer space.
   (C) being widely used for agricultural purposes in greenhouses.
   (D) preventing heat radiation from escaping the earth's atmosphere.

33 What does the scientific community think about the greenhouse effect?

(A) It regards it as an established scientific fact.
(B) It considers it as a promising scientific theory.
(C) It sees it as a useful agricultural technique.
(D) It finds it an important mechanism for removing carbon dioxide from greenhouses.

34 One thing that all atmospheric scientists apparently agree about is that

(A) global temperatures are continually rising.
(B) the amount of carbon dioxide in the atmosphere is increasing.
(C) greenhouses affect the earth's temperature significantly.
(D) the glass of greenhouses has reduced the need to burn as much fuel.

35 Doubts about the greenhouse effect seem to center on the fact that

(A) the earth is steadily cooling down.
(B) growing produce in greenhouses has been only marginally profitable.
(C) it is difficult to locate and identify carbon dioxide in the atmosphere.
(D) past increases in carbon dioxide volume and global temperatures have often not corresponded.

Questions 36–38

Britain is basically a law-abiding country. This may, or may not, explain the addiction of its citizens to crime novels.

36 The first sentence means that, in general, the British people

(A) need few laws.   (C) obey their laws.
(B) need many laws.   (D) disobey their laws.

37 According to the second sentence, the British are noted for

(A) commmitting serious crimes.
(B) legalizing most drugs.
(C) enjoying books about crime.
(D) becoming addicted to drugs.

38 The passage, as a whole, says that the British people ordinarily

(A) disapprove of criminal behavior but enjoy fiction about it.
(B) prefer committing crimes to having to read about such behavior.
(C) are influenced by their literature to obey most of their laws.
(D) disregard their laws, as a rule, because of their reading habits.

Reading Comprehension and Vocabulary

Questions 39–46

A revolution is under way. We are at the dawn of the era of the smart machine – an "information age" that will change forever the way people work, play, travel and even think. Just as the industrial revolution dramatically expanded the strength of man's muscles and the reach of his hand, so the smart-machine revolution will magnify the power of his brain. But unlike the industrial revolution, which depended on finite resources such as iron and oil, the new information age will be fired by a seemingly limitless resource: the inexhaustible supply of knowledge itself.

39 The revolution which this passage says is now under way is occurring in the field of

   (A) travel.
   (B) industry.
   (C) information.
   (D) management.

40 It is claimed that the age of the smart machine

   (A) will soon begin.
   (B) began a few years ago.
   (C) has just begun.
   (D) began with the industrial revolution.

41 The development of the "smart machine" is termed a revolution because it is expected to

   (A) greatly change the way people live.
   (B) finally end the need to work.
   (C) encourage people to play more.
   (D) result in the growth of tourism.

42 The real meaning of lines 3–5 is that the industrial revolution

   (A) made modern man physically much stronger than his ancestors.
   (B) replaced human physical strength with much more powerful machines.
   (C) produced better coordination between the human worker and his tools.
   (D) resulted in the dramatic lengthening of the human arm over time.

43 Sentence 3 (lines 4–6) also indicates that the smart-machine revolution will enable the human brain to

   (A) become larger.
   (B) calculate more quickly.
   (C) understand itself better.
   (D) solve problems more effectively.

44 The whole of sentence 3 is intended basically to show that the benefit to man from the smart-machine revolution
- (A) has already been greater than that from the industrial revolution.
- (B) will one day be greater than that from the industrial revolution.
- (C) is now about the same as that from the industrial revolution.
- (D) will eventually be comparable to that from the industrial revolution.

45 Which of the following was especially important in the development of the industrial revolution?
- (A) Mineral resources.
- (B) Human muscle-power.
- (C) Smart machines.
- (D) Electrical energy.

46 The resource essential to the revolution currently under way is said to be
- (A) oil.
- (B) iron ore.
- (C) knowledge.
- (D) electricity.

Questions 47–48

Guarantee—If you are not satisfied with the quality and/or performance of this product, send name, address and reason for dissatisfaction, along with this entire label and price paid, to the address below. Your purchase price will be returned.

47 Most customers who follow these directions on this product are doing so to
- (A) get back the money they paid for it.
- (B) receive a replacement through the mail.
- (C) obey all the instructions on everything they buy.
- (D) threaten the manufacturer with legal action.

48 Customers following these directions must send the manufacturer
- (A) their receipt from the store.
- (B) the entire product they bought.
- (C) an explanation for their action.
- (D) a stamped, self-addressed envelope.

Questions 49–58

The U.S. Guaranteed Student Loan authority provides federally subsidized 9 per cent loans directly from banks to students. The dependence of Bates College's student body on G.S.L. funds has grown more than sevenfold in the past decade. College officials say this growth is due to the increasing cost of education (tuition and board have more than doubled in ten years, but that is no greater than the inflation rate for the same period) and the shrinking disposable income of the American family. During this period, colleges have tried to accept students without regard to their ability to pay. Thus, Bates's own scholarship fund, from private donations, also increased, from $254,000 in 1970 to $1.4 million in 1981.

49 The first sentence of the passage means that the rate of interest paid on the loans by students (and their families) is

   (A) exactly 9 per cent.
   (B) between 1 and 9 per cent.
   (C) 9 per cent or more.
   (D) sometimes more and sometimes less than 9 per cent.

50 The money for the loans is given to the students by

   (A) their colleges or universities.
   (B) the national government.
   (C) their banks.
   (D) their families.

51 In recent years, use of G.S.L. funds by Bates College's students has apparently increased

   (A) hardly at all.   (C) rather steadily.
   (B) only a little.   (D) very greatly.

52 According to the passage, one important reason for the recent trend in the use of such loans is the fact that

   (A) the number of students has been gradually declining.
   (B) the cost of a university education has been steadily increasing.
   (C) the banks are trying to reduce this kind of business.
   (D) many students have been earning much better grades than before.

53 Another important reason for the recent trend in the use of G.S.L.s is

   (A) a decline in the availability of bank loan money.
   (B) an increase in the availability of bank loan money.
   (C) a decline in the ability of the average American family to pay.
   (D) an increase in the ability of the average American family to pay.

54 According to the article, the increase in the rate of inflation in the U.S. economy over the previous decade was

   (A) much greater than that in the cost of a college education.
   (B) only a little greater than that in the cost of a college education.
   (C) about the same as that in the cost of a college education.
   (D) somewhat less than that in the cost of a college education.

Practice Test I

55 What does the article say (lines 8–9) about students unable to pay for their education at American colleges?

   (A) The colleges tried to increase the number of such students.
   (B) The colleges stopped accepting such students.
   (C) The colleges tried to keep such students in their student bodies.
   (D) The colleges have never had such students in their student bodies.

56 The reason for Bates College's policy on poor students is that college officials believe that students who cannot afford a college education

   (A) are an impossible burden to any college.
   (B) should not be denied the opportunity of a college education if they are academically able.
   (C) should not attempt to apply to Bates College for a free education.
   (D) are unfairly trying to take the place of better qualified students who can pay.

57 The passage makes clear that the scholarship money which Bates College has comes mainly from

   (A) the national government.
   (B) the local community's private banks.
   (C) the personal contributions of private citizens.
   (D) the tuition paid to the college by its student body.

58 Bates College's scholarship fund has increased over the past decade at a rate

   (A) a bit lower than the rate of inflation.
   (B) a bit faster than the rate of inflation.
   (C) much lower than the rate of inflation.
   (D) much faster than the rate of inflation.

Questions 59–60

For each of these questions, choose the answer that is closest in meaning to the original sentence. Note that several of the choices may be factually correct, but you should choose the one that is the closest restatement of the given sentence.

59 Tamble was succeeded by Rose as president.

   (A) Tamble followed Rose as president.
   (B) Rose followed Tamble as president.
   (C) Tamble was more successful as president than Rose.
   (D) Rose was more successful as president than Tamble.

60 Once we'd gotten on the train, we could settle down and relax for the long journey ahead.

Reading Comprehension and Vocabulary

(A) Once we boarded a train and settled down and relaxed for the long journey to come.
(B) After getting on the train, we found it difficult to find a good place to sit and relax for the long journey that followed.
(C) Once upon a time, we got on a train and enjoyed the long trip that followed.
(D) After boarding the train, we managed to find our seats and then to relax on the long trip to come.

DO NOT WORK ON ANY OTHER SECTION OF THE TEST.

IF YOU FINISH IN LESS THAN 45 MINUTES, CHECK
YOUR WORK ON SECTION 3 ONLY. AT THE END OF
45 MINUTES STOP WORK AND CLOSE YOUR TEST BOOK.

Practice Test II

Test of Written English

Time: 30 minutes

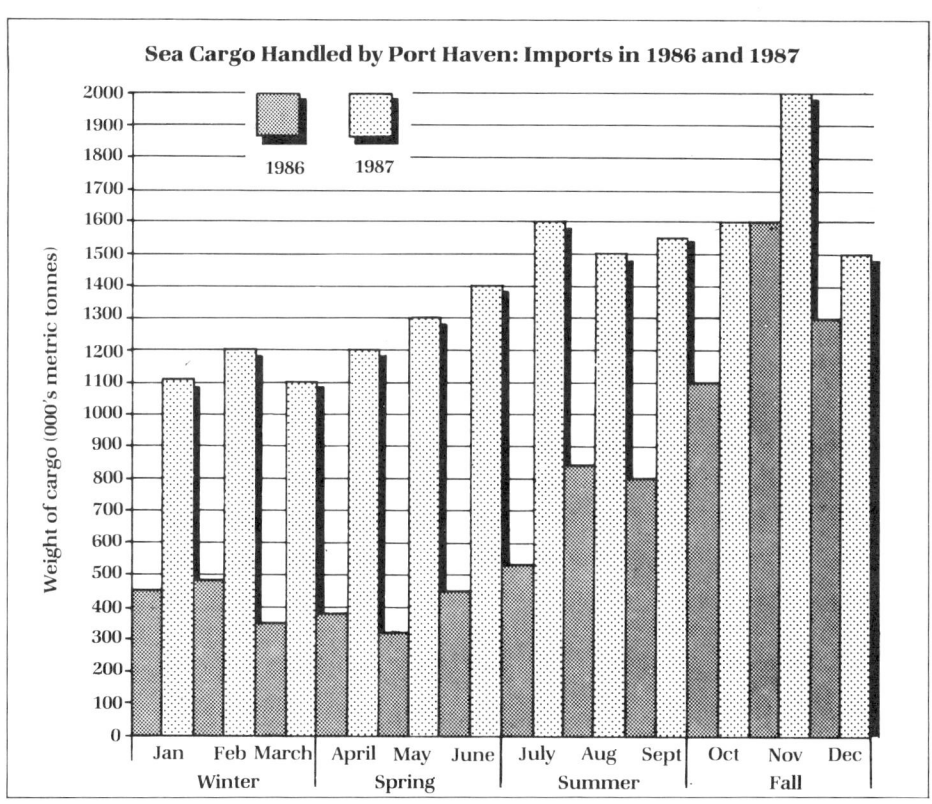

Write a report discussing the changes in the amount of cargo handled by Port Haven in 1986 and 1987, as presented in the above graph. First, compare changes over the four quarters of 1986 and 1987. Second, compare changes for the same four quarters between 1986 and 1987. Lastly, make an overall comparison of the two years.

You may make notes.

27

Practice Test II

Section 1
Listening Comprehension

Time: 40 minutes

In this section of the test, you will have an opportunity to demonstrate your ability to understand spoken English. There are three parts to this section, with special directions for each part.

Part A

Directions: For each problem in Part A, you will hear a short statement. The statements will be spoken just one time. They will not be written out for you, and you must listen carefully in order to understand what the speaker says.

When you hear a statement, read the four sentences in your test book and decide which one is closest in meaning to the statement you have heard. Then, on your answer sheet, find the number of the problem and mark your answer.

    Listen to the following example: Sample Answer

    You will hear: Ⓐ Ⓑ ● Ⓓ

    You will read: (A) Anne doesn't like her brother.
                     (B) Anne usually eats no breakfast.
                     (C) Anne eats a smaller breakfast than her brother.
                     (D) Anne's brother eats as much as she does for breakfast.

Sentence (C), "Anne eats a smaller breakfast than her brother," means most nearly the same as the statement: "Unlike her brother, Anne usually prefers a small breakfast." Therefore, you should choose answer (C).

    Listen to the next example: Sample Answer

    You will hear: Ⓐ ● Ⓒ Ⓓ

    You will read: (A) Mrs. Weller owns a lot of expensive jewelry.

Practice Test II

  (B) Mrs. Weller is wearing a lot of expensive jewelry today.
  (C) Mrs. Weller is lucky to be married to such a wealthy man.
  (D) Mrs. Weller's family owns the biggest jewelry store in town.

Sentence (B), "Mrs. Weller is wearing a lot of expensive jewelry today," is closest in meaning to the sentence: "Mrs. Weller has on a fortune in jewelry." Therefore, you should choose answer (B).

1 (A) The sisters expected dresses as Christmas gifts.
  (B) The sisters wore beautiful clothing on Christmas day.
  (C) The sisters looked around the house for their clothes.
  (D) On Christmas Day, the sisters got dressed quite early.

2 (A) It's expected to be dry, a little windy and cold.
  (B) It's expected to be wet, very windy and warm.
  (C) It's expected to be rainy, a littly windy and cold.
  (D) It's expected to be sunny, very windy and warm.

3 (A) The song will be recorded for the first time.
  (B) The record will be played for the first time.
  (C) The announcer will now perform the song.
  (D) The record will now be played once again.

4 (A) The doctor told us how to treat Joe's back.
  (B) The doctor gave us the name of a good nurse for Joe.
  (C) The doctor recommended a good way to care for Joe.
  (D) The doctor inquired into the reasons for Joe's good health.

5 (A) The players were all wearing neckties.
  (B) The teams ended with the same score.
  (C) The players regularly became tangled up.
  (D) The referees stopped the game early.

6 (A) Mr. Wilson asked if his wife minded watering the lawn.
  (B) Mr. Wilson asked his wife not to forget to water the grass.
  (C) Mrs. Wilson asked her husband if he remembered to water the lawn.
  (D) Mrs. Wilson told her husband she had not yet watered the grass.

7 (A) Linda has very few feelings like other people's.
  (B) Linda has difficulty expressing her feelings for other people.
  (C) Linda appears unconcerned about other people's feelings.
  (D) Linda doesn't respect people who feel sorry for themselves.

Listening Comprehension

8 (A) The police had discovered the criminal hiding at the scene of the crime.
   (B) The police had learned about several crimes.
   (C) The police had obtained useful information at the scene of the crime.
   (D) The police had found almost nothing helpful at the scene of the crime.

9 (A) John likes to visit Yellowstone Park regularly.
   (B) John will probably visit Yellowstone Park next summer.
   (C) John encouraged his friends to visit Yellowstone Park next summer.
   (D) John described his last visit to Yellowstone Park.

10 (A) Mr. Carter asked his wife to pick up his suit at the cleaners.
   (B) Mr. Carter asked his wife to take his suit to the cleaners.
   (C) Mrs. Carter asked her husband to take her suit to the cleaners.
   (D) Mrs. Carter asked her husband to pick up her suit at the cleaners.

11 (A) Sue's school is near Columbia University.
   (B) Sue is going to the Columbia University campus now.
   (C) Sue is in class now at Columbia University.
   (D) Sue is a full-time student at Columbia University.

12 (A) Good-bye.
   (B) We can see you clearly now.
   (C) We expect to watch you on TV.
   (D) We're glad you're looking so well.

13 (A) The next building is for international flights.
   (B) The next place is for ground transportation within the airport.
   (C) The next place is for flights inside the United States.
   (D) The next building is a parking structure.

14 (A) We wanted to know the directions to Rick's new home.
   (B) We wanted Rick to describe his new home for us.
   (C) We wanted Rick to tell us if he liked his new home.
   (D) We wanted Rick to tell us the price of his new home.

15 (A) The referee started the game by blowing his whistle.
   (B) The referee called a foul after blowing his whistle.
   (C) After a player injured himself, the referee stopped the game.
   (D) Blowing his whistle, the referee stopped the play.

16 (A) The food went past Ralph.
   (B) Nancy gave the food to Ralph.
   (C) Ralph handed the food to Nancy.
   (D) The food went past Nancy and Ralph.

17 (A) The people were saved and so was the house.
   (B) Both people and house were lost in the fire.
   (C) The house was saved but the people were lost.
   (D) The people were saved but the house was lost.

18 (A) We didn't buy any apples.
   (B) We took four pounds without paying for them.
   (C) We bought 25 cents' worth of apples.
   (D) We paid $1.00 for apples.

19 (A) The shop still has a lot of copies of the textbook available.
   (B) The shop does not sell textbooks any more.
   (C) Because of slow business, the clerks have left the shop.
   (D) The clerks say that there are only twenty copies of the textbook remaining.

20 (A) John took the elevator to the fifth floor.
   (B) John did most of his writing lying down.
   (C) John wrote five stories while living in this ground-floor apartment.
   (D) John got on five horses before finding one he enjoyed riding.

Part B

Directions: In Part B you will hear fifteen short conversations between two speakers. At the end of each conversation, a third voice will ask a question about what was said. The question will be spoken just one time. After you hear a conversation and the question about it, read the four possible answers and decide which one would be the best answer to the question you have heard. Then, on your answer sheet, find the number of the problem and mark your answer.

Listen to the following example:

You will hear:

You will read: (A) A month
(B) 1½ months.
(C) Two months.
(D) 2½ months.

Sample Answer

Ⓐ Ⓑ Ⓒ ●

From the conversation, we know that the friends will leave in mid-June and return in late August. The best answer, therefore, is (D), "2½ months." So you should choose answer (D).

21 (A) Sell trousers for small boys.
   (B) Make these trousers a bit smaller.
   (C) Exchange the trousers for larger ones.
   (D) Work as a seamstress at this store.

Listening Comprehension

22. (A) Handing the man his boarding pass.
    (B) Pointing to where the man was standing.
    (C) Indicating the way to the plane.
    (D) Picking up the man's boarding pass.

23. (A) Asking for information.
    (B) Filling out a form.
    (C) Applying for a job.
    (D) Registering for classes.

24. (A) How soon they will graduate.
    (B) How much their education costs.
    (C) What kind of job they can get later.
    (D) Which country they will work in later.

25. (A) 5   (B) 8   (C) 11   (D) 14

26. (A) Make the man another lunch.
    (B) Buy the man's lunch for him.
    (C) Get the man a cup of coffee.
    (D) Help look for the man's lunch box.

27. (A) It's closing for the holidays.
    (B) The union is going on strike.
    (C) Car sales have been poor lately.
    (D) The plant is obsolete and unprofitable.

28. (A) He is the office manager.
    (B) He is looking for a new job.
    (C) He will interview the woman.
    (D) He is learning about advertising.

29. (A) They will visit the wife's parents.
    (B) They will visit the woman's home.
    (C) They will visit a lawyer friend.
    (D) They will remain at home.

30. (A) To criticize man's waste of oil.
    (B) To stress that oil is becoming more important.
    (C) To make the woman feel better.
    (D) To demonstrate the importance of the sun.

31. (A) At 6:30.
    (B) At 7:00.
    (C) At 7:30.
    (D) At 8:00.

32. (A) The full price.
    (B) One half of the price.
    (C) One third of the price.
    (D) There was no charge.

33. (A) He was fired.
    (B) He was demoted.
    (C) His salary was reduced.
    (D) Nothing happened to him.

34 (A) Ask for damages in court.
   (B) Buy the children new toys.
   (C) Get herself some new clothes.
   (D) Move to a new neighborhood.

35 (A) Poor.   (C) Rather good.
   (B) Acceptable.   (D) Excellent.

Part C

Directions: In this part of the test, you will hear several short talks and/or conversations. After each talk or conversation, you will be asked some questions. The talks and questions will be said just one time. They will not be written out for you, so you will have to listen carefully in order to understand and remember what the speaker says.

When you hear a question, read the four possible answers in your test book and decide which one would be the best answer to the question you have heard. Then, on your answer sheet, find the number of the problem and fill in (blacken) the space that corresponds to the letter of the answer you have chosen.

Listen to this sample talk:

Now listen to the first question on the sample talk:

You will hear: Sample Answer

You will read: (A) Those emphasizing the   Ⓐ ● Ⓒ Ⓓ
                   profit motive.
               (B) Those reflecting social
                   values he admired.
               (C) Those promoting his
                   religious views.
               (D) Those written by the best
                   fiction writers.

The best answer to the question, "What kind of articles did Mr. Wallace mainly select for his magazine?" is (B), "Those reflecting social values he admired." Therefore, you should choose answer (B).

Now listen to the second question on the sample talk:

You will hear: Sample Answer

You will read: (A) To stress the magazine's   Ⓐ Ⓑ ● Ⓓ
                   lack of seriousness.
               (B) To teach readers many
                   new jokes.
               (C) To indicate Mr. Wallace's
                   love of life.
               (D) To show that non-fiction
                   is funnier than fiction.

Listening Comprehension

The best answer to the question, "What is the speaker's probable purpose in mentioning humor in the *Digest*?" is (C), "To indicate Mr. Wallace's love of life." Therefore, you should choose answer (C).

36 (A) Land at the airport.
    (B) Take a flight for Japan.
    (C) Drive the woman to the hotel.
    (D) Meet a guest at the airport.

37 (A) At a hotel.
    (B) At the airport.
    (C) At the man's house.
    (D) At the woman's house.

38 (A) Mr. Tanaka's arrival.
    (B) The man's departure.
    (C) A hotel reception.
    (D) A business conference.

39 (A) To repay Mr. Tanaka's kindness.
    (B) To get invited back to Tokyo.
    (C) To increase the hotel's business.
    (D) To keep the manager's admiration.

40 (A) She failed.
    (B) She barely passed.
    (C) She passed easily.
    (D) She wouldn't say.

41 (A) Changing lanes.
    (B) Starting on a hill.
    (C) Parking at the curb.
    (D) Keeping a proper distance.

42 (A) Not using her signal.
    (B) Being in the wrong lane.
    (C) Driving too slowly.
    (D) Not looking over her shoulder.

43 (A) It hit her from behind.
    (B) She rolled backwards.
    (C) She shifted into reverse.
    (D) She went through a red light.

44 (A) To describe that day's weather.
    (B) To warn people of possible danger.
    (C) To give the regular weather report.
    (D) To stop the program momentarily.

45 (A) North.
    (B) South.
    (C) East.
    (D) West.

46 (A) The lightning.
    (B) Heavy rainfall.
    (C) Possible tornadoes.
    (D) The gusts of wind.

47 (A) In the kitchen.
    (B) In the bathroom.
    (C) In the garage.
    (D) In the basement.

48 (A) To spectators in a stadium.
    (B) To a caller on the phone.
    (C) To a customer picking up tickets.
    (D) To listeners on the radio or TV.

49 (A) The tickets are sold from machines.
   (B) The staff are all out to lunch.
   (C) It is after normal working hours.
   (D) Every staff member is very busy.

50 (A) Hockey.
   (B) Baseball.
   (C) Football.
   (D) Basketball.

THIS IS THE END OF THE LISTENING COMPREHENSION PORTION OF THE TEST. LOOK AT THE TIME NOW, BEFORE YOU BEGIN WORK ON SECTION 2. USE *EXACTLY 25 MINUTES* TO WORK ON SECTION 2.

Section 2
Structure and Written Expression

Time: 25 minutes

This section is designed to measure your ability to recognize language that is appropriate for standard written English. There are two types of questions in this section, with special directions for each type.

Part A

Directions: Questions 1–15 are incomplete sentences. Four words or phrases, marked (A), (B), (C), (D), are given beneath each sentence. You are to choose the one word or phrase that best completes the sentence. Then, on your answer sheet, find the number of the problem and mark your answer.

Example I.

We got a lot of exercise during our holiday in the Swiss Alps ----- skiing every day.

(A) to
(B) by
(C) in
(D) on

Sample Answer
Ⓐ ● Ⓒ Ⓓ

In English, the sentence should read, "We got a lot of exercise during our holiday in the Swiss Alps by skiing every day." Therefore, you should choose (B).

Example II.

Los Angeles never gets snowstorms and Honolulu -----.

(A) is too.
(B) does too.
(C) isn't either.
(D) doesn't either.

Sample Answer
Ⓐ Ⓑ Ⓒ ●

The sentence should read, "Los Angeles never gets snowstorms and Honolulu doesn't either." Therefore, you should choose (D).

As soon as you understand the directions, begin work on the problems.

1 Do you know where ----- when you met him this morning?

(A) Dave went
(B) was Dave going
(C) Dave was going
(D) did Dave go

2 That young man still denies ----- the fire behind the store.

   (A) to start
   (B) having started
   (C) to starting
   (D) having been started

3 Professor Lockwood recommended that Juan ----- in chemistry.

   (A) not major
   (B) wouldn't major
   (C) not to major
   (D) isn't majoring

4 It is expected that ----- be as many as 50,000 spectators for today's air show.

   (A) it will
   (B) they could
   (C) there might
   (D) perhaps may

5 ----- New York City is America's largest city, it is not the capital of New York State; Albany is.

   (A) Despite
   (B) Although
   (C) Because of
   (D) In spite of

6 ----- of fire, many more buildings were destroyed than the earthquake itself had damaged.

   (A) Consequence
   (B) Consequently
   (C) Consequences
   (D) As a consequence

7 All right, Johnny, it's time you ----- to bed.

   (A) went
   (B) would go
   (C) will be going
   (D) going to go

8 Ivan ----- hasn't repaired his bicycle tire.

   (A) yet
   (B) soon
   (C) still
   (D) already

9 A chemist prepares his experiments carefully before trying to carry ------ in his laboratory.

   (A) it out
   (B) out it
   (C) them out
   (D) out them

10 Here in today's paper it says the zoo has just obtained ----- animal no one has ever heard of before.

   (A) a
   (B) the
   (C) any
   (D) some

11 ----- that land was known as Siam but its modern name is Thailand.

   (A) Origin
   (B) Original
   (C) Originates
   (D) Originally

Structure and Written Expression

12 That book looks like an advanced ----- text to me.

   (A) economic   (C) economist
   (B) economics   (D) economical

13 It's probable both that there were many severe storms in this area ----- ships sank.

   (A) so many   (C) and many
   (B) that many   (D) and that many

14 Does this package belong to ----- or is it yours?

   (A) we   (B) us   (C) our   (D) ours

15 If you don't want to get wet, then you had better ----- this umbrella with you.

   (A) take   (C) to take
   (B) for taking   (D) taken

Part B

Directions: In questions 16–40 each sentence has four words or phrases underlined. The four underlined parts of the sentence are marked (A) (B), (C), (D). You are to identify the one underlined word or phrase that should be corrected or rewritten. Then, on your answer sheet, find the number of the problem and mark your answer.

Example I.   Sample Answer

   One of Mrs. Wilson's <u>daughters</u> <u>doesn't</u> play   Ⓐ Ⓑ ● Ⓓ
                             A   B
   the piano as <u>skillful</u> as the other one <u>does</u>.
                     C   D

Answer (C), the underlined adjective <u>skillful</u>, would not be accepted in carefully written English. The adverb <u>skillfully</u> should be used instead. Therefore, the sentence should read: "One of Mrs. Wilson's daughters doesn't play the piano as skillfully as the other one does." To answer the problem correctly, you would choose (C).

Example II.   Sample Answer

   The woman <u>said</u> she <u>had saw</u> the robbery   Ⓐ ● Ⓒ Ⓓ
                   A   B
   <u>take place</u> <u>on</u> the previous day.
       C   D

Answer (B), the underlined phrase <u>had saw</u>, should not be used in carefully written English. The form <u>seen</u> should be used after <u>had</u>. Therefore, the sentence should read, "The woman said she had seen the robbery take place on the previous day." To answer the problem correctly, you would choose (B).

Practice Test II

As soon as you understand the directions, begin work on the problems.

16 Winston Churchill, that was Britain's Prime Minister during World War
                      A   B   C
    II, was also a noted author.
                D

17 The rate of inflation is soon expecting to decrease gradually by some
          A   B   C   D
    economists.

18 The sisters' mother bought her two new dresses each.
        A   B C   D

19 The American public feels very concerning about pollution of
         A   B
    underground water sources by industrial and agricultural chemicals.
       C   D

20 In the end of the party, Lois found herself doing the dishes alone again,
    A   B   C
    as usual.
      D

21 One simple means of making tea is just for pouring hot water over a tea
              A   B   C   D
    bag.

22 The government is considering to pass a law making it a crime to carry
                  A   B   C
    any kind of small, easily hidden handgun.
                    D

23 The Smiths are very proud of that their son always gets high marks in his
                         A   B   C
    courses.
      D

24 We called the baseball park up to ask that when the game was scheduled
                          A   B   C
    to begin that afternoon.
          D

25 The American Indians killed the buffalo only when necessity to obtain
                 A   B   C
    food, clothing and shelter.
        D

Structure and Written Expression

26 Some relatives of mine like staying at their cabin on Lake Omega every
                      A   B   C
    summer holidays they get.
           D

27 Do not try to walk to the university from here because it is about 10 miles
    A   B   C
    far.
    D

28 Reporting the news from foreign countries are the responsibility of a
              A   B   C   D
    foreign correspondent.

29 By calling the new world was India, Columbus was quite mistaken in his
                          A   B   C D
    geography.

30 Oil has been an extremely important to modern industrial society.
    A   B   C   D

31 The minister of agriculture blamed the lower vegetable production for
                   A   B
    insufficient rainfall last summer.
                 C   D

32 During his eye examination, Mr. Stevenson first closed the eyes and then
               A   B   C
    opened them.
    D

33 A teacher is responsible of the progress of his or her students.
                 A   B   C   D

34 Results from many researchers' studies would seem to suggest that
                      A   B
    the average human adult needs between seven to nine hours of sleep per
                  C   D
    night.

35 Everyone is awaiting to see if the Titanic will ever be raised from
                A   B   C
    the ocean bottom.
    D

Practice Test II

36 In the richest countries, the average person expects to live to over 70
       A   B   C
    years of old.
          D

37 Tropical rain forests everywhere are being rapidly destroyed, but many
       A   B
    officials express no concern for the people and animals depending on it.
                                C   D

38 Clearly, that is wiser to be safe than to be sorry.
       A   B   C   D

39 Why so many high school students graduate weak in reading and
         A   B
    mathematics are questions continuing to disturb American educators.
                  C   D

40 Pleasing with their new car, the Levines went for a short drive around
       A   B   C   D
    the town.

DO NOT WORK ON ANY OTHER SECTION OF THE TEST.

IF YOU FINISH IN LESS THAN 25 MINUTES,
CHECK YOUR WORK ON SECTION 2 ONLY. AT THE
END OF 25 MINUTES, GO ON TO SECTION 3.
USE *EXACTLY 45 MINUTES* TO WORK ON SECTION 3.

Section 3
Reading Comprehension and Vocabulary

Time: 45 minutes

There are two types of questions in this section, with special directions for each type.

Part A

Directions: In questions 1–30 each sentence has a word or phrase underlined. Below each sentence are four other words or phrases. You are to choose the one word or phrase which would best keep the meaning of the original sentence if it were substituted for the underlined word or phrase. Look at the example.

Example.   Sample Answer

The lecture hall is practically full now.   Ⓐ Ⓑ ● Ⓓ

(A) half   (C) almost
(B) hardly   (D) completely

The best answer is (C), because the sentence, "The lecture hall is almost full now," is closest in meaning to the original sentence, "The lecture hall is practically full now." Therefore, you should mark answer (C).

As soon as you understand the directions, begin work on the problems.

1 Everyone who heard the story found it incredible.

  (A) irresistible   (C) immaterial
  (B) unbelievable   (D) nonsensical

2 You must ask the authorities for that information.

  (A) writers   (C) officials
  (B) artists   (D) engineers

3 Jack said that it was essential to leave immediately.

  (A) unwise   (C) desirable
  (B) possible   (D) necessary

4 There were many rumors going around about the mayor's private life, but in a subsequent speech he denied them all.

   (A) a long
   (B) a fine
   (C) a later
   (D) an angry

5 Ultimately, the better team did not win the game.

   (A) Eventually
   (B) Fortunately
   (C) Occasionally
   (D) Presumably

6 The men are negotiating over the sale of the diamonds.

   (A) arguing
   (B) fighting
   (C) thinking
   (D) bargaining

7 Everyone knows that the couple were reluctant to have their daughter marry Mr. Townsend.

   (A) eager
   (B) pleased
   (C) unwilling
   (D) disappointed

8 These machines have been idle for the past month.

   (A) been troublesome
   (B) not been serviced
   (C) been working well
   (D) not been running at all

9 We hope there will be sufficient food tonight.

   (A) tasty
   (B) enough
   (C) varied
   (D) perfect

10 Mary's immediate objective could not be readily seen.

   (A) bias
   (B) goal
   (C) subject
   (D) direction

11 Smith was told he would have to relinquish most of his property to his former wife.

   (A) give up
   (B) pay back
   (C) show off
   (D) carry out

12 The police are still looking for those assassins.

   (A) killers
   (B) robbers
   (C) burglars
   (D) hijackers

13 Ellen said she would accompany Dave if she had time.

   (A) go with
   (B) call up
   (C) write to
   (D) come for

Reading Comprehension and Vocabulary

14 His previous play won a literary prize.

   (A) best   (C) earlier
   (B) first   (D) lengthy

15 Let me reiterate my main point.

   (A) repeat   (C) revise
   (B) report   (D) review

16 We could get no information about what had happened to the captives.

   (A) pirates   (C) patients
   (B) prisoners   (D) passengers

17 The news is that those animals in the zoo will be released soon.

   (A) sold   (C) put on display
   (B) freed   (D) returned to their cages

18 Judge Jones' decisions are generally regarded as being equitable.

   (A) fair   (C) clever
   (B) long   (D) popular

19 Mr. Carson thought he was entitled to more assistance from the government.

   (A) had received   (C) had a right to
   (B) would obtain   (D) might apply for

20 The march of scientific progress has been relentless during the twentieth century.

   (A) wonderful   (C) unstoppable
   (B) unexpected   (D) astonishing

21 Is it true that insulin can now be synthesized?

   (A) produced artificially   (C) tested safely
   (B) injected frequently   (D) taken orally

22 Some observers thought the war would be calamitous.

   (A) marvelous   (C) tremendous
   (B) hazardous   (D) disastrous

23 The Winfields are a quite conventional family.

   (A) cheerful   (C) humorous
   (B) ordinary   (D) well-known

24 The young couple continued their secret rendezvous last week.

  (A) courses (C) messages
  (B) meetings (D) conversations

25 Officials making those statements asked not to be identified.

  (A) questioned (C) named
  (B) quoted (D) blamed

26 The lawyer conceded that Mrs. Taylor's statement was true.

  (A) proved (C) doubted
  (B) denied (D) admitted

27 It is now definite that school will reopen on the fifth of September.

  (A) likely (C) certain
  (B) presumed (D) doubtful

28 Richard was always a fine athlete as a young man.

  (A) son (C) salesman
  (B) student (D) sportsman

29 Is the Canadian dollar equivalent to the U.S. dollar?

  (A) about the same in value as (C) worth a bit more than
  (B) very different in value from (D) worth a bit less than

30 Some of the business practices of that chemical company make it a menace in this area.

  (A) large employer (C) leader
  (B) major producer (D) threat

Part B

Directions: The remaining questions in this section are based on a variety of reading material (single sentences, paragraphs, advertisements, and the like). In questions 31–60, you are to choose the one best answer, (A), (B), (C), or (D), to each question. Then, on your answer sheet, find the number of the problem and mark your answer. Answer all questions following a passage on the basis of what is stated or implied in that passage.

Read the following sample passage.

   Normally, the human body combats an infection by producing antibodies to the invading disease. These seek out the intruder and destroy it. These antibodies persist in the bloodstream for long periods and prevent reinfection.

Reading Comprehension and Vocabulary

Example I.

The passage says that the main function of antibodies is to

Sample Answer

Ⓐ Ⓑ Ⓒ ●

(A) attack the human body.
(B) invade other organisms.
(C) produce other antibodies.
(D) fight invading diseases.

The passage says that the body fights (combats) disease by producing antibodies. Therefore, you should choose answer (D).

Example II:

The article says that, after an infection from a particular disease has been cured, the antibodies

Sample Answer

Ⓐ Ⓑ ● Ⓓ

(A) all disappear.
(B) continue to increase.
(C) remain in the blood.
(D) gradually decline in number.

The passage says that the antibodies remain (persist) in the blood for a long time and prevent the disease from recurring. Therefore, you should choose (C) as the best completion of the sentence.

As soon as you understand the directions, begin work on the problems.

Questions 31–32

Officials of the micro-electronics industry are fond of remarking that had the automobile industry improved its technology at the same rate computer science has, it now would be turning out Rolls-Royces that cost no more than $70 apiece.

31 Officials in the micro-electronics industry are really saying that computer technology

(A) has improved at about the same rate as that of the auto industry.
(B) has developed much faster than that of the auto industry.
(C) has developed somewhat more slowly than that of the auto industry.
(D) cannot be compared, as to rate of change, with that of the auto industry.

32 Why do officials of the micro-electronics industry like to make the remark reported in the above passage?

(A) They hope that Rolls-Royces will soon cost about $70.
(B) They are disappointed because computers do not yet cost $70.
(C) They are pleased at the price decline in micro-electronic goods.
(D) They are critical of the recent price increases of most cars.

Questions 33–35

Up to now, there has been no logically consistent way in which the gold price could be forecast with any confidence. Gold experts have generally relied on various statistical methods to extrapolate historical data into the future. Then they applied intuitive value judgments to arrive at a discount for the sake of conservatism.

33 Historically, how have gold experts forecast the gold price?
- (A) With consistency and with confidence in their predictions.
- (B) With neither consistency nor confidence in their predictions.
- (C) Inconsistently but with confidence in their forecasts.
- (D) Rather consistently but without very much confidence in their forecasts.

34 In making their predictions, how have the gold experts used statistics?
- (A) They have averaged the price of the previous few years.
- (B) They have depended heavily on current prices to calculate future ones.
- (C) They have devised new formulas especially for the gold market.
- (D) They have tried to anticipate price changes on the basis of past experience.

35 What has been the usual result of the experts' intuitive value judgments?
- (A) To use more complex statistical measures in their work.
- (B) To lower their predictions for the expected gold price.
- (C) To give their best customers a discount on their purchases.
- (D) To become gradually less conservative in making predictions.

Questions 36–41

The computer age is producing an army of robots – machines that are directed by electronic brains and which replace human labor in industrial operations. Many are artificial arms which reach into areas man enters only at his peril, such as the inside of a nuclear reactor.

Already in 1980 there were over 8000 such robots working in industrial plants throughout the world. The big changeover to the robot, however, is likely to come only when their costs go down while workers' wages continue to rise.

36 Sentence 1 indicates that robots are used mainly
- (A) to fight wars.
- (B) to operate computers.
- (C) to direct electronic brains.
- (D) to take the place of human workers.

Reading Comprehension and Vocabulary

37 An observer today is most likely to see robots in operation in

   (A) military battles.
   (B) modern factories.
   (C) business offices.
   (D) scientific laboratories.

38 The shape of many robots already in use is somewhat similar to that of a human

   (A) brain.   (B) arm.   (C) hand.   (D) foot.

39 The article makes clear that a very valuable use of many robots is to

   (A) act as a teacher to human beings.
   (B) replace the human brain in producing computers.
   (C) aid doctors in medical operations.
   (D) do tasks extremely dangerous for humans to do.

40 Which one of the following statements about the last sentence in the passage is <u>certainly</u> true?

   (A) Robots are becoming cheaper all the time.
   (B) The cost of a human worker is higher than that of the average robot.
   (C) Robots are becoming more expensive all the time.
   (D) The cost of the average robot is higher than that of a human worker.

41 The writer indicates that the widespread replacement of human labor by industrial robots

   (A) has already begun worldwide.
   (B) is starting especially in the developing nations.
   (C) is being delayed mainly for economic reasons.
   (D) will not take place before the end of this century.

Questions 42–48

With its ready supply of hydropower from the Merrimack River, Lowell, Massachusetts, 30 miles from Boston, quickly became a major textile center in the early 1800's. It drew thousands of New England farm girls and, later, waves of immigrants, to labor twelve hours a day in its red-brick mills and factories. By the 1920's most of the mills had closed or moved south, and Lowell fell into an economic abyss that deepened for more than four decades. Now, however, the "birthplace of the American industrial revolution" is prospering once again – and providing a model of restoration and revival for other blighted New England mill towns.

42 Originally, the energy to run Lowell's factories came mostly, if not entirely, from

   (A) hydroelectric facilities.

(B) burning coal which had been imported.
(C) petroleum.
(D) a combination of local power sources.

43 Most of the factories were engaged in the production of

(A) machine tools.
(B) clothing.
(C) processed food.
(D) vehicles.

44 The passage says that a large proportion of its workers in the early 19th century apparently were

(A) young women from the surrounding rural areas.
(B) middle-aged men who had recently lost their jobs.
(C) young men with little or no education.
(D) people of all ages from many foreign countries.

45 If laborers with a typical working day had to work six full days a week, how many hours a week could they expect to be on the job?

(A) About 40.
(B) About 55.
(C) About 70.
(D) About 85.

46 After a century of operation, the majority of Lowell's mills and factories

(A) were no longer in business in Lowell.
(B) had grown more prosperous than ever before.
(C) began manufacturing different products.
(D) recruited many new workers from foreign lands.

47 Until a few years ago, the effects of the changes that occurred in the 1920's resulted in an economy in Lowell that

(A) became weaker and weaker.
(B) has remained unchanged for about sixty years.
(C) grew somewhat more prosperous than before.
(D) has been envied by the rest of the United States.

48 The passage considers current economic changes in Lowell important because

(A) it was the birthplace of the American industrial revolution.
(B) its workers are willing to work longer hours than those in nearby towns.
(C) it has suddenly developed many new serious economic problems.
(D) it provides a good example to nearby towns of how to overcome their similar problems.

Reading Comprehension and Vocabulary

Questions 49–52

An American multi-national firm has an immediate opening for a trilingual receptionist. Small switchboard. Excellent French and English, good German. Must have experience and be reliable, punctual, present good appearance. Please send current photograph, detailed CV, and salary requirements to Box 441, c/o this newspaper.

49 One important piece of information NOT included in this advertisement is

   (A) the kind of person required.
   (B) the nature of the position.
   (C) the location of the firm.
   (D) the date when the position will be available.

50 According to the ad, all of the following will probably be required regularly of a successful applicant EXCEPT

   (A) answering the phone.
   (B) greeting visitors to the firm.
   (C) using several languages fluently.
   (D) preparing correspondence and memos.

51 Requirements of the successful applicant will include all of the following EXCEPT

   (A) arriving regularly on time.
   (B) wearing appropriate clothing.
   (C) being concerned with quality performance.
   (D) having native fluency in three languages.

52 It is clear from the ad that the company will give important weight to each applicant's

   (A) nationality and mother tongue.
   (B) place of residence.
   (C) education and work background.
   (D) marital status.

Questions 53–58

Experts emphasize that senility is not an inevitable result of the ageing process, like graying hair. It is a specific disease with a variety of causes, resulting in failing memory, a decline in the ability to work with numbers, errors in judgment, and irritability often leading to paranoia.

By their 70s, many normal people show some decline in memory, reasoning, learning and problem-solving, but others do not. Older people with a good deal of education who are used to using their minds appear to have less difficulty. Moreover, about 15–20 per cent of patients who become senile suffer from conditions that can be corrected.

53 From the passage, it is clear that senility is a problem affecting especially a person's

   (A) hair.   (B) mind.   (C) skin.   (D) blood.

54 The passage states that senility seems to affect mainly

   (A) men.   (C) the young.
   (B) women.   (D) the elderly.

55 Experts point out that senility

   (A) can generally be prevented.
   (B) can generally be cured.
   (C) does not affect everybody.
   (D) has no specific symptoms.

56 Which of the following is not described as a sign of senility?

   (A) Graying hair.   (C) Errors in judgment.
   (B) Failing memory.   (D) Confusion with numbers.

57 All of the following are indicators of approaching senility EXCEPT

   (A) a modest decline in learning ability.
   (B) serious errors in judgment.
   (C) a frequent loss of memory.
   (D) extreme irritability leading to paranoia.

58 Which one of the following statements based on the last sentence in the reading is true?

   (A) Most people become senile.
   (B) Most people do not become senile.
   (C) Most senile people can be cured.
   (D) Most senile people can not be cured.

Questions 59–60

For each of these questions, choose the answer that is closest in meaning to the original sentence. Note that several of the choices may be factually correct, but you should choose the one that is the closest restatement of the given sentence.

59 There's not a single corner of Ireland that my friends haven't visited.

   (A) My friends have visited only a single part of Ireland.
   (B) My friends haven't visited any parts of Ireland yet.
   (C) My friends have visited most parts of Ireland already.
   (D) My friends have visited every part of Ireland already.

Reading Comprehension and Vocabulary

60 As dried yeast is approximately three times as strong as fresh yeast, it is only necessary to use from one-third to one-half of the amount of fresh yeast.

- (A) If it seems that the fresh yeast is not quite as strong as the dried yeast, one need only use a third to a half as much of it.
- (B) One need use only a third to a half as much dried yeast as fresh yeast since the former is around three times stronger than the latter.
- (C) Whenever it is necessary to choose between fresh and dried yeast, the latter should be used in amounts only a third or a half as much as the former.
- (D) It is only necessary to use between a third and a half as much fresh yeast as dried yeast, since the former is about three times stronger than the latter.

DO NOT WORK ON ANY OTHER SECTION OF THE TEST.

IF YOU FINISH IN LESS THAN 45 MINUTES, CHECK YOUR WORK ON SECTION 3 ONLY. AT THE END OF 45 MINUTES STOP WORK AND CLOSE YOUR TEST BOOK.

Practice Test III

Test of Written English

Time: 30 minutes

Television is often described as a great technological invention. Others criticize television, avoid watching it too much, and may forbid their children from watching certain programs. Explain some of the arguments for each side. Say which point of view you agree with and why.

You may make notes.

Practice Test III

Section 1
Listening Comprehension

Time: 40 minutes

In this section of the test, you will have an opportunity to demonstrate your ability to understand spoken English. There are three parts to this section, with special directions for each part.

Part A

Directions: For each problem in Part A, you will hear a short statement. The statements will be spoken just one time. They will not be written out for you, and you must listen carefully in order to understand what the speaker says.

When you hear a statement, read the four sentences in your test book and decide which one is closest in meaning to the statement you have heard. Then, on your answer sheet, find the number of the problem and mark your answer.

Listen to the following example: **Sample Answer**

You will hear: Ⓐ Ⓑ ● Ⓓ

You will read: (A) Anne doesn't like her brother.
(B) Anne usually eats no breakfast.
(C) Anne eats a smaller breakfast than her brother.
(D) Anne's brother eats as much as she does for breakfast.

Sentence (C), "Anne eats a smaller breakfast than her brother," means most nearly the same as the statement: "Unlike her brother, Anne usually prefers a small breakfast." Therefore, you should choose answer (C).

Listen to the next example: **Sample Answer**

You will hear: Ⓐ ● Ⓒ Ⓓ

You will read: (A) Mrs. Weller owns a lot of expensive jewelry.

54

(B) Mrs. Weller is wearing a lot of expensive jewelry today.
(C) Mrs. Weller is lucky to be married to such a wealthy man.
(D) Mrs. Weller's family owns the biggest jewelry store in town.

Sentence (B), "Mrs. Weller is wearing a lot of expensive jewelry today," is closest in meaning to the sentence: "Mrs. Weller has on a fortune in jewelry." Therefore, you should choose answer (B).

1 (A) Mary prefers going to the clinic alone.
  (B) Mary doesn't want to go to the clinic today.
  (C) Mary would rather go to the clinic today than stay home.
  (D) Mary hopes her friend will go to the clinic with her.

2 (A) At least one third of the items on sale have been sold.
  (B) All prices are now as much as one third lower than before.
  (C) One third of all the items in the store are on sale.
  (D) Prices on some items are as much as 67 per cent lower.

3 (A) Lim's is on Main not far from 8th.
  (B) Lim's is on 8th not far from Main.
  (C) Lim's is on Main next to the bank building.
  (D) Lim's is at the corner of 8th and Main.

4 (A) Can I borrow your flashlight?
  (B) Do you have matches or a lighter?
  (C) What's the matter? Can't you see very well?
  (D) Do you have a spare light bulb you can give me?

5 (A) The Eliots say they enjoy their week ends.
  (B) The Eliots will stay with us this week end.
  (C) The Eliots will phone us on Saturday or Sunday.
  (D) The Eliots are coming for supper Saturday evening.

6 (A) Let's look for falling rocks.
  (B) Don't let those falling rocks hit you.
  (C) Help me move these rocks which fell.
  (D) Look out the window at those falling rocks.

7 (A) A patient must take pills for this condition.
  (B) A patient should have an inoculation for this condition.
  (C) A patient needs neither pills nor shots for this condition.
  (D) A patient can choose either pills or shots for this condition.

Listening Comprehension

8 (A) Mr. and Mrs. Crenshaw prefer driving on winding rural roads.
   (B) Neither Mr. nor Mrs. Crenshaw sleeps while the other drives.
   (C) Mr. and Mrs. Crenshaw help each other with the driving.
   (D) Mr. and Mrs. Crenshaw try to stay mainly on superhighways.

9 (A) Mary Ann has been waiting for Mr. Weber a long time.
   (B) Mary Ann is sorry Mr. Weber was very late.
   (C) Mary Ann says Mr. Weber called to say he will be delayed.
   (D) Mary Ann is sorry that she made Mr. Weber wait for her.

10 (A) The children's behavior is discourteous.
   (B) The children are learning to perform in public.
   (C) The children are unable to act.
   (D) The children sit very quietly without playing.

11 (A) Steve told the salesman he didn't like the motorcycle.
   (B) Steve said he preferred another motorcycle to the BMW.
   (C) While admiring the BMW motorcycle, Steve said he would buy it.
   (D) Steve said he did not have enough money to buy the motorcycle.

12 (A) The government gave the village many good tractors.
   (B) The villagers ordered a lot of tractors from a company.
   (C) The village gratefully received two tractors from the government.
   (D) The government at last laid railroad tracks to the village.

13 (A) Elizabeth's dress is beautiful.
   (B) Elizabeth's dress isn't beautiful.
   (C) Is Elizabeth's dress beautiful?
   (D) Isn't Elizabeth's dress beautiful?

14 (A) The teacher never knows which twin is which.
   (B) The twins do not tell the teacher their names.
   (C) The twins like to play a joke on the teacher.
   (D) The teacher knows which twin is which but shares the secret with them.

15 (A) The light suddenly exploded.
   (B) Suddenly the light bulb burst into flame.
   (C) The light started a fire in the ceiling.
   (D) The bulb was no good any more.

16 (A) The shop will pay for it.
   (B) The manager will pay for it.
   (C) The cashier has to pay for it.
   (D) The customers pay through higher prices.

17 (A) Fred is older than Dennis.
   (B) Fred is about nine.

(C) Dennis is about nine.
   (D) Dennis is three times older than Fred.

18 (A) The French and the British joined forces to fight the American Indians.
   (B) The American Indians and the British joined forces to fight the French.
   (C) The American Indians and the French joined forces to fight the British.
   (D) All three sides were fighting against one another.

19 (A) I think Sandra is unwell.
   (B) Sandra told me she is not well.
   (C) Sandra said she has been feeling chilly.
   (D) Sandra said the weatherman predicts colder weather is coming.

20 (A) The salesman refused to change the price of the suit.
   (B) Changes to the suit were included in the price.
   (C) The tailor had no time to make changes to the suit.
   (D) Mr. Ford decided not to take the suit after all.

Part B

Directions: In Part B you will hear fifteen short conversations between two speakers. At the end of each conversation, a third voice will ask a question about what was said. The question will be spoken just one time. After you hear a conversation and the question about it, read the four possible answers and decide which one would be the best answer to the question you have heard. Then, on your answer sheet, find the number of the problem and mark your answer.

Listen to the following example:

You will hear: Sample Answer

You will read: (A) A month.   Ⓐ Ⓑ Ⓒ ●
               (B) 1½ months.
               (C) Two months.
               (D) 2½ months.

From the conversation, we know that the friends will leave in mid-June and return in late August. The best answer, therefore, is (D), "2½ months." Therefore you should choose answer (D).

21 (A) A butcher.   (C) A carpenter.
   (B) A plumber.   (D) An electrician.

Listening Comprehension

22 (A) Preparing for bed.
   (B) Walking toward the campus.
   (C) Looking for a place to live.
   (D) Inviting some friends to visit.

23 (A) He has lost his job.
   (B) He has received a promotion.
   (C) He has been transferred abroad.
   (D) He has been scolded for making a mistake.

24 (A) That it was too expensive.
   (B) That with utilities it was high.
   (C) That without utilities it was not high.
   (D) That he didn't have to pay for utilities.

25 (A) She gave him his dollar back.
   (B) Two quarters and a half dollar.
   (C) Two quarters and fifty pennies.
   (D) Three quarters, two dimes and a nickel.

26 (A) He probably supports nuclear power plants.
   (B) He probably opposes nuclear power plants.
   (C) He probably has no opinion on this topic.
   (D) He probably tries to understand both sides.

27 (A) Take some more vegetables.
   (B) Pass the woman the meat.
   (C) Avoid taking any more food.
   (D) Help to prepare the potatoes.

28 (A) His wife.   (C) A store detective.
   (B) A saleslady.   (D) A customs official.

29 (A) She hasn't been well lately.
   (B) She feels unhappy without the TV.
   (C) She wants an expert to repair it.
   (D) She wants him to fix it at once.

30 (A) He doesn't care for that brand.
   (B) He has just finished a cigarette.
   (C) He isn't seated in the smoking section.
   (D) He doesn't like to smoke cigarettes.

31 (A) Someone hired by the auto club.
   (B) No one. He repaired it himself.
   (C) A private mechanic he phoned.
   (D) A passing police patrol car.

32 (A) He approves of the action.
   (B) He feels sorry for those students.
   (C) He considers the punishment excessive.
   (D) He has no opinion about the action.

33 (A) The waitress will eat it there.
   (B) The waitress will take it home.
   (C) The restaurant will throw it away.
   (D) The couple will take it home.

34 (A) Pay with his credit card.
   (B) Go home to get his money.
   (C) Get some money from his wife.
   (D) Pay for his purchase by check.

35 (A) A burglary.   (C) An organization.
   (B) An operation.   (D) An armed robbery.

Part C

Directions: In this part of the test, you will hear several short talks and/or conversations. After each talk or conversation, you will be asked some questions. The talks and questions will be spoken just one time. They will not be written out for you, so you will have to listen carefully in order to understand and remember what the speaker says.

When you hear a question, read the four possible answers in your test book and decide which one would be the best answer to the question you have heard. Then, on your answer sheet, find the number of the problem and fill in (blacken) the space that corresponds to the letter of the answer you have chosen.

Listen to this sample talk:

Now listen to the first question on the sample talk:

You will hear: Sample Answer

You will read: (A) Those emphasizing the   Ⓐ ● Ⓒ Ⓓ
                   profit motive.
               (B) Those reflecting social
                   values he admired.
               (C) Those promoting his
                   religious views.
               (D) Those written by the best
                   fiction writers.

The best answer to the question, "What kind of articles did Mr. Wallace mainly select for his magazine?" is (B), "Those reflecting social values he admired." Therefore, you should choose answer (B).

Listening Comprehension

Now listen to the second question on the sample talk:

You will hear: Sample Answer

You will read: (A) To stress the magazine's   Ⓐ Ⓑ ● Ⓓ
lack of seriousness.
(B) To teach readers many
new jokes.
(C) To indicate Mr. Wallace's
love of life.
(D) To show that non-fiction
is funnier than fiction.

The best answer to the question, "What is the speaker's probable purpose in mentioning humor in the *Digest*?" is (C), "To indicate Mr. Wallace's love of life." Therefore, you should choose answer (C).

36 (A) A pedestrian.   (C) A policeman.
   (B) A taxi driver.   (D) The store manager.

37 (A) She must walk one more block.
   (B) She must walk two more blocks.
   (C) She must drive one more mile.
   (D) She must drive two more miles.

38 (A) Driving her to the store.
   (B) Giving her directions to the store.
   (C) Waiting on her in the store.
   (D) Describing the appearance of the store.

39 (A) Fluid.   (C) Protein.
   (B) Salt.   (D) Starch.

40 (A) Not to do it at all.   (C) To do it with a friend.
   (B) Not to begin it rapidly.   (D) To follow it carefully.

41 (A) Sugar.   (C) Fluids.
   (B) Fat.   (D) Proteins.

42 (A) By adding fat.   (C) By adding proteins.
   (B) By adding muscle.   (D) By adding fluids.

43 (A) That there was no effect.
   (B) That it improved operations.
   (C) That operations became less efficient.
   (D) That the employees became dissatisfied.

44 (A) As unusually good.   (C) As not very good.
   (B) As quite ordinary.   (D) As unsatisfactory.

Practice Test III

45 (A) The shift among employees.
   (B) Her friendship with the staff.
   (C) Her own hard work.
   (D) The new record-keeping system.

46 (A) To notify her of her promotion.
   (B) To inform her of new equipment.
   (C) To inquire about office problems.
   (D) To discuss meetings of the board.

47 (A) He was not an honest businessman.
   (B) To bring in a better sales manager.
   (C) He wants to work for another firm.
   (D) To take over sales in another area.

48 (A) It's about the same.
   (B) It's nearly as good.
   (C) It's a little better.
   (D) It's much better now.

49 (A) First.   (C) Third.
   (B) Second.   (D) Fourth.

50 (A) As having little significance.   (C) As a promotion for him.
   (B) As a bad business decision.   (D) As a kind of punishment.

THIS IS THE END OF THE LISTENING
COMPREHENSION PORTION OF THE TEST.
LOOK AT THE TIME NOW, BEFORE YOU
BEGIN WORK ON SECTION 2. USE
EXACTLY 25 MINUTES TO WORK ON
SECTION 2.

Section 2
Structure and Written Expression

Time: 25 minutes

This section is designed to measure your ability to recognize language that is appropriate for standard written English. There are two types of questions in this section, with special directions for each type.

Part A

Directions: Questions 1–15 are incomplete sentences. Four words or phrases, marked (A), (B), (C), (D), are given beneath each sentence. You are to choose the one word or phrase that best completes the sentence. Then, on your answer sheet, find the number of the problem and mark your answer.

Example I.

We got a lot of exercise during our holiday in the Swiss Alps ----- skiing every day.

(A) to
(B) by
(C) in
(D) on

Sample Answer
(A) ● (C) (D)

In English, the sentence should read, "We got a lot of exercise during our holiday in the Swiss Alps by skiing every day." Therefore, you should choose (B).

Example II.

Los Angeles never gets snowstorms and Honolulu -----.

(A) is too.
(B) does too.
(C) isn't either.
(D) doesn't either.

Sample Answer
(A) (B) (C) ●

The sentence should read, "Los Angeles never gets snowstorms and Honolulu doesn't either." Therefore, you should choose (D).

As soon as you understand the directions, begin work on the problems.

1 My friend would not tell me ----- for his new car.

   (A) how much he paid   (C) how much did he pay
   (B) how he paid much   (D) how he'd pay very much

2 The sign said that unauthorized persons were prohibited ----- that restricted area.

   (A) entering
   (B) to enter
   (C) from entering
   (D) not to enter

3 The reason for the traffic accident was ----- one of the drivers had lost control of his car.

   (A) why   (B) when   (C) that   (D) how

4 The Eiffel Tower is still ----- of the man-made structures in the world.

   (A) a very high one
   (B) highest one
   (C) one of the highest
   (D) the higher one

5 Our house ----- on a large plot of land.

   (A) lies
   (B) sits
   (C) rests
   (D) stands

6 The more people chopped down the trees, -----.

   (A) the erosion became very bad
   (B) the worse the erosion became
   (C) the erosion became much worse
   (D) the worsening erosion caused much difficulty

7 Problems common to most countries include the social, economic and -----.

   (A) politics
   (B) political
   (C) government
   (D) of government

8 The corner market is ----- only until 8:30 pm.

   (A) opening
   (B) opens
   (C) opened
   (D) open

9 Corporal Jackson, you will obey this order ----- now!

   (A) as   (B) just   (C) only   (D) right

10 My friend said she is very eager ----- a real Hollywood star.

   (A) to meet
   (B) in meeting
   (C) for meeting
   (D) that she can meet

11 Don't worry about her; she just feels like staying home ----- tonight.

   (A) lone
   (B) alone
   (C) lonely
   (D) lonelier

Structure and Written Expression

12 Prior to our conference, the executive director had requested that everyone ----- well prepared.

(A) is
(B) be
(C) was
(D) will be

13 Many ----- items are turned in to the railroad officials every week.

(A) lose   (B) loss   (C) lost   (D) losing

14 It's been officially announced already that the new ship ----- to be named the Southern Cross.

(A) is   (B) can   (C) will   (D) does

15 The best way to get from Tokyo to Yokohama quickly is by -----.

(A) train
(B) a train
(C) trains
(D) some trains

Part B

Directions: In questions 16–40 each sentence has four words or phrases underlined. The four underlined parts of the sentence are marked (A), (B), (C), (D). You are to identify the one underlined word or phrase that should be corrected or rewritten. Then, on your answer sheet, find the number of the problem and mark your answer.

Example I.   Sample Answer

One of Mrs. Wilson's daughters doesn't play
                A   B
the piano as skillful as the other one does.
              C   D

Answer (C), the underlined adjective skillful, would not be accepted in carefully written English. The adverb skillfully should be used instead. Therefore, the sentence should read: "One of Mrs. Wilson's daughters doesn't play the piano as skillfully as the other one does." To answer the problem correctly, you would choose (C).

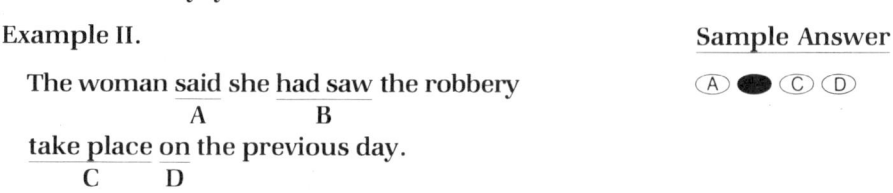

Example II.   Sample Answer

The woman said she had saw the robbery
            A   B
take place on the previous day.
    C   D

Answer (B), the underlined phrase had saw, should not be used in carefully written English. The form seen should be used after had. Therefore, the sentence should read, "The woman said she had seen the robbery take place on the previous day." To answer the problem correctly, you would choose (B).

Practice Test III

As soon as you understand the directions, begin work on the problems.

16 Randolph is the boy scored the winning points for his school
                     A   B   C
   basketball team.
          D

17 Henry likes to get up early tomorrow morning, to start fishing before the
          A   B   C   D
   sun rises.

18 The luxury cars in the showroom were quickly sold out, despite of their
              A   B   C   D
   high prices.

19 A professional sports team can be very profitable as long as too many
                    A   B   C
   people buy tickets for every game.
                          D

20 Almost of the trees in this plantation have had to be cut down and burned
      A   B   C   D
   as a result of the infestation.

21 If man were less greedy, more animal species could be avoided
       A   B   C   D
   extinction.

22 The police is holding four young men in jail and charging them with
              A   B   C   D
   selling illegal drugs.

23 After we have finished supper, let's all go to downtown to see a movie.
              A   B   C   D

24 Looking in his mirror, Roy could see a bus following in the back of his
              A   B   C   D
   car.

25 Early Monday morning the director discovered that some valuable pieces
      A   B   C
   of equipment was missing from his laboratory.
                  D

26 It is very possible that the horses will frightened if there is suddenly a loud
            A   B   C   D
   noise.

Structure and Written Expression

27 It is often claimed that all good things come at last to he who is patient
               A   B   C
    and waits for them.
                   D

28 As you know that water is a compound produced from the reaction
                    A   B   C   D
    between hydrogen and oxygen.

29 The 12-year-old girl is more prettier than her older sisters.
             A   B   C   D

30 Jane was worried that the newsstand would have run out of copies of the
                  A   B
    evening paper by the time she got there, but she found that it still had
                                             C
    very much left.
             D

31 In no other country there are as many people as in China.
                 A   B   C   D

32 The director eventually told the young actress that he would have her in
                       A   B
    the lead female role of his new movie and none else.
           C   D

33 To balance next year's budget, the government needs either to increase
           A   B
    taxes or it has to cut spending.
               C   D

34 Before going to abroad, Mr. Peters received special training to help him
                   A   B
    to do his job better.
     C   D

35 From a chemical standpoint, a number of materials would be suitable for
                                    A
    our purposes; for examples, take gold or silver, metals which are very
                     B   C
    stable but too expensive to be practical.
                           D

36 Some time next week, we will fix the roof, as well as painting the outside
                A   B   C   D
    of the house.

37 Members of the US Congress like to meet often with the people who elect
              A   B   C
   them, so they return back to their communities regularly.
                        D

38 Suddenly, Katherine gave a shriek and rushed into the kitchen, where
      A   B   C
   she could smell her cakes burn.
                           D

39 One of the fishermen was describing for the listeners around him how a
             A   B
   huge large wave nearly turned his boat over.
        C   D

40 Richard Nixon resigned from his high office, still claimed that he
                                                A   B
   had done nothing wrong.
      C   D

DO NOT WORK ON ANY OTHER SECTION OF THE TEST.

IF YOU FINISH IN LESS THAN 25 MINUTES,
CHECK YOUR WORK ON SECTION 2 ONLY. AT THE
END OF 25 MINUTES, GO ON TO SECTION 3.
USE *EXACTLY 45 MINUTES* TO WORK ON SECTION 3.

Section 3
Reading Comprehension and Vocabulary

Time: 45 minutes

There are two types of questions in this section, with special directions for each type.

Part A

Directions: In questions 1–30 each sentence has a word or phrase underlined. Below each sentence are four other words or phrases. You are to choose the one word or phrase which would best keep the meaning of the original sentence if it were substituted for the underlined word or phrase. Look at the example.

Example.   Sample Answer

The lecture hall is practically full now.   Ⓐ Ⓑ ● Ⓓ

(A) half   (C) almost
(B) hardly   (D) completely

The best answer is (C), because the sentence, "The lecture hall is almost full now," is closest in meaning to the original sentence, "The lecture hall is practically full now." Therefore, you should mark answer (C).

As soon as you understand the directions, begin work on the problems.

1 The doctor said Larry's main problem was obesity.

   (A) being fat   (C) smoking too much
   (B) getting old   (D) exercising too little

2 Did anyone acknowledge responsibility for the outbreak of the fire?

   (A) admit   (C) find out
   (B) report   (D) inquire about

3 My friends in Singapore frequently visit the United States.

   (A) often   (C) seldom
   (B) never   (D) sometimes

4 It is not likely that John will come this weekend.

   (A) hoped   (C) probable
   (B) correct   (D) expected

Practice Test III

5 They say the government is subsidizing the shipping industry.
   - (A) trying to destroy
   - (B) helping to support
   - (C) starting to develop
   - (D) continuing to operate

6 We thought Jane's performance was particularly good.
   - (A) especially
   - (B) unbelievably
   - (C) necessarily
   - (D) unexpectedly

7 The child has been relatively silent most of this evening.
   - (A) sadly
   - (B) strangely
   - (C) remarkably
   - (D) comparatively

8 I periodically get a letter from my old friends in Delhi.
   - (A) often
   - (B) never
   - (C) rarely
   - (D) sometimes

9 Please let me know right away when you hear the news.
   - (A) at once
   - (B) at home
   - (C) by noon
   - (D) by phone

10 You can see their portraits in this room.
   - (A) prices
   - (B) products
   - (C) pictures
   - (D) purchases

11 That firm was affiliated with a soft-drinks company.
   - (A) owned by
   - (B) founded by
   - (C) associated with
   - (D) reorganized with

12 We still must decide on beverages for this evening.
   - (A) things to eat
   - (B) things to drink
   - (C) things to wear
   - (D) things to do

13 The ideas of that religious group were denounced on yesterday evening's program on TV.
   - (A) praised
   - (B) ignored
   - (C) attacked
   - (D) explained

14 I saw to it that the work was finished on time.
   - (A) made sure
   - (B) found
   - (C) could prove
   - (D) was informed

69

Reading Comprehension and Vocabulary

15 What guarantee do we have of this product's quality?

   (A) possibility   (C) indication
   (B) knowledge   (D) assurance

16 The main result of the meeting was unanimity.

   (A) great anger   (C) total agreement
   (B) great concern   (D) total confusion

17 The neighbors left their homes simultaneously.

   (A) in a great hurry   (C) all of a sudden
   (B) at the same time   (D) once and for all

18 Mrs. Davis said she did not know what might alleviate her pain.

   (A) cause   (C) ease
   (B) stop   (D) prevent

19 Marie said she wished to express her gratitude to the Wilsons.

   (A) condolences   (C) dissatisfaction
   (B) appreciation   (D) congratulations

20 John soon learned that his time in the 100-meter race had been quite an accomplishment.

   (A) a cancellation   (C) an achievement
   (B) a complication   (D) an accompaniment

21 Manuel had his first opportunity to attend a baseball game when he was only six.

   (A) wish   (C) ticket
   (B) chance   (D) luck

22 It is a fact that Henry is quite rigid in his views.

   (A) tolerant   (C) inflexible
   (B) arrogant   (D) inaccurate

23 Harold showed a picture of his bride to his friends.

   (A) new firm   (C) new garden
   (B) new horse   (D) new wife

24 The present regime took over only last August.

   (A) council   (C) commander
   (B) principal   (D) government

Practice Test III

25 <u>Incidentally</u>, did you hear that Joyce has just had a baby?

  (A) By the way
  (B) For your information
  (C) Actually
  (D) Personally

26 Last Friday Barton left his office <u>for good</u>.

  (A) hastily
  (B) casually
  (C) contentedly
  (D) permanently

27 John's parents told him always to be <u>courteous</u>.

  (A) neat
  (B) kind
  (C) honest
  (D) polite

28 The Dennisons have decided to buy a new home <u>in the country</u>.

  (A) in the nation
  (B) in a rural area
  (C) in a large city
  (D) in a nearby county

29 Mr. Thompson has been <u>a diplomat</u> for over forty years.

  (A) a president of a university
  (B) a representative of his government
  (C) a leader of a symphony orchestra
  (D) a doctor specializing in children's problems

30 Few people at first were able to see the <u>magnitude</u> of Africa's food problems.

  (A) size
  (B) limit
  (C) cause
  (D) solution

Part B

Directions: The remaining questions in this section are based on a variety of reading material (single sentences, paragraphs, advertisements, and the like). In questions 31–60, you are to choose the one best answer, (A), (B), (C), or (D), to each question. Then on your answer sheet, find the number of the problem and mark your answer. Answer all questions following a passage on the basis of what is stated or implied in that passage.

Read the following sample passage.

Normally, the human body combats an infection by producing antibodies to the invading disease. These seek out the intruder and destroy it. These antibodies persist in the bloodstream for long periods and prevent reinfection.

Example I.   Sample Answer

  The passage says that the main function of   Ⓐ Ⓑ Ⓒ ●
  antibodies is to

71

Reading Comprehension and Vocabulary

    (A) attack the human body.
    (B) invade other organisms.
    (C) produce other antibodies.
    (D) fight invading diseases.

The passage says that the body fights (combats) disease by producing antibodies. Therefore, you should choose answer (D).

Example II: Sample Answer

    The article says that, after an infection from   Ⓐ Ⓑ ● Ⓓ
    a particular disease has been cured, the
    antibodies

    (A) all disappear.
    (B) continue to increase.
    (C) remain in the blood.
    (D) gradually decline in number.

The passage says that the antibodies remain (persist) in the blood for a long time and prevent the disease from recurring. Therefore, you should choose (C) as the best completion of the sentence. Now continue.

As soon as you understand the directions, begin work on the problems.

Questions 31–33

    The newspaper industry today is infected by an adventurous spirit, and many publishers are willing to give expensive technological innovations a try. Two considerations are probably tipping the balance: skyrocketing labor and material costs, and fears of eventual competition from electronic media.

31 Sentence 1 means that, in the modern newspaper business,

    (A) workers enjoy experiencing adventures.
    (B) workers are easily infected by disease.
    (C) owners compete to buy the most expensive machinery.
    (D) owners want to make use of the most recent inventions.

32 The phrase in sentence 2, "tipping the balance," in this passage means

    (A) upsetting newspaper officials.
    (B) encouraging workers to strike.
    (C) making owners willing to spend a lot of money.
    (D) causing readers to buy many more newspapers than before.

33 Newspaper publishers are concerned about all of the following EXCEPT

    (A) labor costs.   (C) the electronic media.
    (B) material costs.   (D) their adventurous spirit.

Questions 34–39

In most animals, dental decay is a rare problem. In man, and especially in the affluent West, the disease has reached epidemic proportions.

The cause of tooth decay in human beings is a bacterium that feeds on the sugar in our food. It digests the sugar more easily by converting it into an acid. The acid then dissolves the enamel, the outer coating of the teeth, and finally attacks the living nerve within. The result is the agonizing pain we know as toothache.

34 According to the passage, how common is it for animals to suffer from tooth decay?

(A) They never suffer from it.
(B) They seldom suffer from it.
(C) They suffer from it as commonly as people do.
(D) They suffer from it more commonly than people do.

35 What does the passage say about the problem of tooth decay in the rich Western countries?

(A) It is steadily decreasing each year.
(B) It has remained unchanged for a long time.
(C) It has been increasing slowly for years.
(D) It is now virtually out of control.

36 Human teeth decay when they are attacked by a kind of

(A) sugar.
(B) acid.
(C) nerve.
(D) food.

37 Decay cannot begin until the bacterium produces

(A) food from sugar.
(B) sugar from food.
(C) acid from sugar.
(D) sugar from acid.

38 The term "tooth decay" refers to the

(A) digestion of the food.
(B) conversion of the sugar.
(C) production of the acid.
(D) dissolution of the enamel.

39 The last sentence means that toothache is a condition which is often

(A) unbearable.
(B) quite unexpected.
(C) a bit unpleasant.
(D) unpleasant but bearable.

Questions 40–43

For most of Western history, the mark of the educated person was to know the best of what had been thought and written, to be able to think critically, and to be morally discerning and esthetically discriminating.

Reading Comprehension and Vocabulary

Today, however, American universities teach whatever students want to learn. In 1978, for example, fewer than 20 per cent of all undergraduate degrees were awarded in the humanities – literature, language, history, philosophy and other liberal studies. Education, in short, is a buyer's market, and what most students want is not a philosophy of life but a salable skill.

40 In the past, according to the writer of the passage, all of the following were considered important characteristics of a truly educated person EXCEPT

  (A) knowledge of the great writings.
  (B) ability to earn a good income.
  (C) ability to think critically.
  (D) appreciation of fine art.

41 The author's definition of the humanities would include study of all of the following subjects EXCEPT

  (A) poetry.   (C) foreign languages.
  (B) philosophy.   (D) civil engineering.

42 The term from the reading which is closest in meaning to the word "humanities" is

  (A) Western history.   (C) buyer's market.
  (B) liberal studies.   (D) salable skills.

43 It appears that the main academic concern of today's average American student is

  (A) knowing some useful foreign languages.
  (B) being sure to get a job after graduation.
  (C) establishing a sound personal moral code.
  (D) having a deep appreciation for great art.

Questions 44–49

Subscription Service

Please include the address portion of your wrapper to ensure prompt service whenever you write to us about your subscription. And if you're moving, please let us know four weeks before changing your address. Just place address portion of wrapper where indicated and print your new address below.

Mail to: Division Magazine Subscriber Service, Division Square, Oakland Street, Jefferson City, Oklahoma 99984

To subscribe: Mail this form with your payment and indicate:

☐ 1. New subscription

☐ 2. Renew my subscription

☐ 3. Payment enclosed

☐ 4. Bill me later

ATTACH YOUR ADDRESS LABEL HERE

Name _____

(please print)

Address _____

_____

Country _____

Reading Comprehension and Vocabulary

44 The main purpose of this notice in Division Magazine is to help

(A) the magazine inform subscribers of its publishing plans.
(B) readers correspond with the magazine about their subscriptions.
(C) subscribers inform the magazine about their travel plans.
(D) the magazine correspond with readers who buy it at the newsstand.

45 The address portion of the wrapper is attached to this notice by only those readers who

(A) wish to renew their subscriptions.
(B) are arranging for new subscriptions.
(C) wish to end their subscriptions.
(D) buy their copies at the newsstand.

46 Subscribers expecting a change of address are asked to inform the magazine of this fact around

(A) 10 days in advance.
(B) 20 days in advance.
(C) 30 days in advance.
(D) 40 days in advance.

47 The reason the magazine asks subscribers planning to move to inform it of that fact is to

(A) be sure the magazine gets its money.
(B) have subscribers pay after their move.
(C) avoid interruptions in serving its readers.
(D) have this information for purposes of marketing research.

48 The address to be printed below the place for the label is

(A) the magazine's old address.
(B) the magazine's new address.
(C) the subscriber's old address.
(D) the subscriber's new address.

49 If you wished to subscribe to Division Magazine and inserted ONLY THIS FORM into your envelope, which boxes should you have checked in the form?

(A) Boxes 1 and 3.
(B) Boxes 2 and 3.
(C) Boxes 1 and 4.
(D) Boxes 2 and 4.

Questions 50–57

Hawaii, which has no fossil fuels, was hit hard by the oil shocks of the early 1970s. Even today 92 per cent of its energy needs are met by imported oil. But Hawaii has made impressive gains in energy conservation by recycling bagasse, the damp brown waste left over after sugar cane has been milled and its juices extracted.

Until recently, the bagasse was largely wasted. But in the 1970s, the state's sugar growers dramatically increased their use of it as fuel for electric-generating plants. Compressed into pellets, they discovered, one pound yields about 80 per cent of the energy of a pound of coal. Today, Hawaiian sugar plantations produce enough energy to run themselves, and they sell enough excess electricity to utilities to meet 7 per cent of the state's total energy needs.

50 The "impressive gains" that the article says Hawaii has made include all of the following EXCEPT

(A) beginning to find energy substitutes for oil.
(B) saving money on energy imports from abroad.
(C) finding an important use for a former waste product.
(D) earning more money for its annual sugar crop.

51 In Hawaii, bagasse is today being "recycled" in the sense that it is

(A) being plowed under to fertilize the land.
(B) rotated in the mill while being pressed.
(C) not being grown every year as was formerly true.
(D) no longer being thrown away as useless.

52 The article makes clear that interest in the use of bagasse was spurred, when it was, by

(A) a severe agricultural crisis.
(B) the rising cost of petroleum.
(C) the need to increase oil imports.
(D) the growing volume of sugar exports.

53 When reprocessed into fuel, the form of the bagasse most closely resembles which of the following?

(A) Lumps of coal.   (C) Small hard peas.
(B) A clear liquid like water. (D) Wooden boards.

54 After being reprocessed, the bagasse is used mostly to

(A) generate electricity.
(B) produce more sugar.
(C) replace coal as a fuel.
(D) help get rid of other waste products.

55 The economic advantages of recycling bagasse were certainly increased by the fact that, pound for pound, bagasse yields

(A) as much energy as oil.
(B) nearly as much energy as coal.
(C) more energy than oil.
(D) almost 80 per cent more energy than coal.

Reading Comprehension and Vocabulary

56 Nowadays, Hawaii's sugar growers can produce enough bagasse to

   (A) export a large part of their bagasse crop.
   (B) make state fertilizer imports unnecessary.
   (C) meet most of the state's energy requirements.
   (D) be self-sufficient in filling their own energy needs.

57 How are most of the power demands of Hawaii's people met?

   (A) By the state's sugar growers.
   (B) By foreign sugar-exporting companies.
   (C) By the state's own oil producers.
   (D) By the state's utility firms.

Questions 58–60

For each of these questions, choose the answer that is <u>closest in meaning</u> to the original sentence. Note that several of the choices may be factually correct, but you should choose the one that is the closest <u>restatement of the given sentence</u>.

58 If it hadn't been for that timely announcement to evacuate the building, there could have been many more casualties.

   (A) The announcement caused many more casualties than would otherwise have occurred.
   (B) Because of the announcement, there were no casualties at all.
   (C) As a result of the announcement, very few casualties occurred.
   (D) Without the announcement, quite a few more casualties might have occurred.

59 The teams have hardly gotten under way with the game.

   (A) They've barely started the game.
   (B) They've barely finished the game.
   (C) They've started the game with difficulty.
   (D) They've finished the game with difficulty.

60 The auto industry's concern with pollution control has given way to fuel economy as the top priority.

   (A) The auto industry is equally concerned about pollution control and fuel economy.
   (B) Pollution control is no longer an important concern of the auto industry but fuel economy is.
   (C) Fuel economy has replaced pollution control as the auto industry's principal concern.
   (D) Fuel economy, while still important, is not as much of a concern to the auto industry as is pollution control.

DO NOT WORK ON ANY OTHER SECTION OF THE TEST.

IF YOU FINISH IN LESS THAN 45 MINUTES, CHECK YOUR WORK ON SECTION 3 ONLY. AT THE END OF 45 MINUTES STOP WORK AND CLOSE YOUR TEST BOOK.

Practice Test IV

Test of Written English

Time: 30 minutes

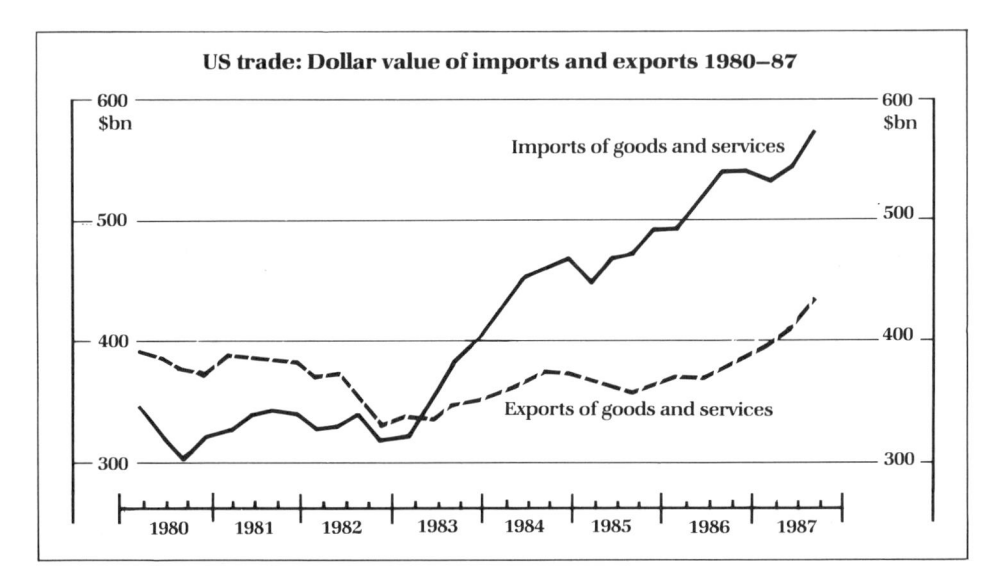

US trade: Dollar value of imports and exports 1980–87

(Graph showing imports of goods and services and exports of goods and services, in $bn, from 1980 to 1987. Imports range roughly from 300 to nearly 600 $bn; exports range roughly from 300 to 400 $bn.)

Look at the above graph of the dollar value of US imports and exports for the years 1980–87, noting trade surpluses and deficits and those quarters of highest and lowest imports and exports.

In general, is it better for a company or country to buy more than it sells, or vice versa? Why? Explain briefly the importance for the US economy of the trends shown in the graph.

You may make notes.

Practice Test IV

Section 1
Listening Comprehension

Time: 40 minutes

In this section of the test, you will have an opportunity to demonstrate your ability to understand spoken English. There are three parts to this section, with special directions for each part.

Part A

Directions: For each problem in Part A, you will hear a short statement. The statements will be spoken just one time. They will not be written out for you, and you must listen carefully in order to understand what the speaker says.

When you hear a statement, read the four sentences in your test book and decide which one is closest in meaning to the statement you have heard. Then, on your answer sheet, find the number of the problem and mark your answer.

Listen to the following example: Sample Answer

You will hear: Ⓐ Ⓑ ● Ⓓ

You will read: (A) Anne doesn't like her brother.
(B) Anne usually eats no breakfast.
(C) Anne eats a smaller breakfast than her brother.
(D) Anne's brother eats as much as she does for breakfast.

Sentence (C), "Anne eats a smaller breakfast than her brother," means most nearly the same as the statement: "Unlike her brother, Anne usually prefers a small breakfast." Therefore, you should choose answer (C).

Listen to the next example: Sample Answer

You will hear: Ⓐ ● Ⓒ Ⓓ

You will read: (A) Mrs. Weller owns a lot of expensive jewelry.

81

Practice Test IV

      (B) Mrs. Weller is wearing a lot of expensive jewelry today.
      (C) Mrs. Weller is lucky to be married to such a wealthy man.
      (D) Mrs. Weller's family owns the biggest jewelry store in town.

Sentence (B), "Mrs. Weller is wearing a lot of expensive jewelry today," is closest in meaning to the sentence: "Mrs. Weller has on a fortune in jewelry." Therefore, you should choose answer (B).

1 (A) Of course, Jim thought his friend was wise.
   (B) Jim requested advice from his friend.
   (C) Jim said his friend's action wasn't wise.
   (D) Jim wanted his friend to be more careful.

2 (A) The report could not be sent.
   (B) The reporter was accused of lying.
   (C) The report was cut or changed in many places.
   (D) The reporter was ordered to leave the country.

3 (A) Be careful not to stumble while getting off.
   (B) Please look at the steps while getting off.
   (C) Go down the steps in order to get off.
   (D) Please do not keep other passengers waiting to get off.

4 (A) Mr. Washburn helped his daughter count her used checks.
   (B) Mr. Washburn and his daughter started a new account at the bank.
   (C) Mr. Washburn's daughter asked him to check her account.
   (D) Together Mr. Washburn and his daughter checked how many places were open.

5 (A) Mr. Baker sold his cookies door-to-door.
   (B) We could taste some cookies without paying.
   (C) The bakery still sells some cookies cheaply.
   (D) The baker's best cookies are the chocolate ones.

6 (A) Frank expects to be praised as a fine driver.
   (B) The court will probably send Frank to jail.
   (C) The judge will probably take away Frank's license.
   (D) Frank will probably have to pay a lot of money.

7 (A) The company has greatly increased the number of new products.
   (B) The companies have increased their profits 100 per cent.
   (C) Most companies have had a very profitable year.

Listening Comprehension

    (D) This company's profits are three times higher this year than last year.

8 (A) The baby has been sleeping well lately.
   (B) The baby's parents have had to wake him often recently.
   (C) The baby has been waking up his parents often lately.
   (D) The baby's parents have had to sleep at different times recently.

9 (A) Mr. Rawlins asked his wife to make him a birthday cake.
   (B) Mr. Rawlins bought his wife a birthday cake.
   (C) Mrs. Rawlins asked her husband to get her a birthday cake.
   (D) Mrs. Rawlins bought her husband a birthday cake.

10 (A) Uncle Sam said that people should not talk too much.
    (B) Uncle Sam said that people should not be too serious.
    (C) Uncle Sam said that people should consider the feelings of others.
    (D) Uncle Sam said that people should discuss intellectual topics.

11 (A) The official wanted Amy to back the car up.
    (B) The official wanted Amy to drive back to his office.
    (C) The official wanted Amy to look behind her in the mirror.
    (D) The official wanted Amy to raise her head a little higher.

12 (A) Mr. Clinton easily gets lost while driving to his friends' homes.
    (B) Mr. Clinton doesn't take the most direct way to his friends' homes.
    (C) Mr. Clinton does more for his friends than they expect of him.
    (D) Mr. Clinton avoids doing any more for his friends than is necessary.

13 (A) The next bus should leave around 2:45.
    (B) The next bus should leave around 3:15.
    (C) The next bus should leave around 3:45.
    (D) The next bus should leave around 4:30.

14 (A) Professor Higgins forgets his students' names.
    (B) Professor Higgins doesn't know his students' names.
    (C) Professor Higgins repeatedly asks his students their names.
    (D) Professor Higgins calls his students by the wrong names.

15 (A) Students in most teachers' classes were attending regularly.
    (B) The principal said he would attend several teachers' classes soon.
    (C) Teachers were told by the dissatisfied principal to warn students about attendance.
    (D) The principal angrily told the students to attend class regularly.

16 (A) Everyone can sit down at that table.
    (B) Everyone can carry a chair to that table.
    (C) Everyone can take a chair away from that table.

Practice Test IV

    (D) Everyone can remain seated at that table.

17 (A) Daniel's parents are the same height.
    (B) Daniel is as tall as his father is.
    (C) Daniel is almost as tall as his mother.
    (D) Daniel's father is taller than he is.

18 (A) Gary lent $100 to each cousin.
    (B) Gary borrowed $100 from each cousin.
    (C) All three borrowed $100 each from a bank.
    (D) One of Gary's cousins lent $100 to the other.

19 (A) Calvin has a scholarship this semester.
    (B) Calvin almost got a scholarship last semester.
    (C) Even with good marks, Calvin did not get a scholarship this semester.
    (D) With good marks this semester, Calvin might get a scholarship next semester.

20 (A) That man hit my arm as he passed.
    (B) That man said something odd as he passed.
    (C) I think I have seen that man somewhere before.
    (D) Having too many strangers around makes me feel uncomfortable.

Part B

Directions: In Part B you will hear fifteen short conversations between two speakers. At the end of each conversation, a third voice will ask a question about what was said. The question will be spoken just one time. After you hear a conversation and the question about it, read the four possible answers and decide which one would be the best answer to the question you have heard. Then, on your answer sheet, find the number of the problem and mark your answer.

    Listen to the following example:

    You will hear: **Sample Answer**

    You will read: (A) A month.   (A) (B) (C) ●
                        (B) 1½ months.
                        (C) Two months.
                        (D) 2½ months.

From the conversation, we know that the friends will leave in mid-June and return in late August. The best answer, therefore, is (D), "2½ months." So you should choose answer (D).

21 (A) His phone wasn't working.   (C) She couldn't be at home.
    (B) Her phone wasn't working.   (D) Her husband wasn't at home.

Listening Comprehension

22 (A) Mr. Weiner. (C) Dr. Muller.
   (B) Mrs. Weiner. (D) Mrs. Pennington.

23 (A) The man.
   (B) She herself.
   (C) The two of them together.
   (D) The store's gift-wrapping department.

24 (A) Look for beverages in the lobby.
   (B) Get some fresh air outside.
   (C) Walk around the auditorium.
   (D) Stay in their seats.

25 (A) As identification to cash a check.
   (B) To prove he is a foreign visitor.
   (C) The woman is an immigration official.
   (D) In order to obtain a visa.

26 (A) They are both studying for M.A.s.
   (B) They are both working.
   (C) He is studying while she works.
   (D) She is studying while he works.

27 (A) By bus. (C) By subway.
   (B) By taxi. (D) In their own car.

28 (A) Pull it out. (C) Put in a large filling.
   (B) Do a little drilling. (D) Do nothing since it's healthy.

29 (A) No, because he is too busy. (C) They have not yet asked him.
   (B) Yes, even though he is busy. (D) Henry has not decided yet.

30 (A) Florist. (C) Organist.
   (B) Dentist. (D) Pharmacist.

31 (A) Satisfied with their price.
   (B) Displeased with their quality.
   (C) Pleased with modern mass-production techniques.
   (D) Dissatisfied with their technological complexity.

32 (A) He was dead.
   (B) He was alive but unable to walk.
   (C) He was playing golf once again.
   (D) He could walk only with crutches.

33 (A) Pass around cans of beer. (C) Throw away the empty cans.
   (B) Open the first can of beer. (D) Carry the cans from the car.

Practice Test IV

34 (A) To invite the man to join them.
   (B) To suggest politely that he leave.
   (C) To offer to let him help cook.
   (D) To encourage him to have another drink.

35 (A) 6   (B) 12   (C) 18   (D) 24

Part C

Directions: In this part of the test, you will hear several short talks and/or conversations. After each talk or conversation, you will be asked some questions. The talks and questions will be said just one time. They will not be written out for you, so you will have to listen carefully in order to understand and remember what the speaker says.

When you hear a question, read the four possible answers in your test book and decide which one would be the best answer to the question you have heard. Then, on your answer sheet, find the number of the problem and fill in (blacken) the space that corresponds to the letter of the answer you have chosen.

Listen to this sample talk:

Now listen to the first question on the sample talk:

You will hear: Sample Answer

You will read: (A) Those emphasizing the   Ⓐ ● Ⓒ Ⓓ
                    profit motive.
               (B) Those reflecting social
                    values he admired.
               (C) Those promoting his
                    religious views.
               (D) Those written by the best
                    fiction writers.

The best answer to the question, "What kind of articles did Mr. Wallace mainly select for his magazine?" is (B), "Those reflecting social values he admired." Therefore, you should choose answer (B).

Now listen to the second question on the sample talk:

You will hear: Sample Answer

You will read: (A) To stress the magazine's   Ⓐ Ⓑ ● Ⓓ
                    lack of seriousness.
               (B) To teach readers many
                    new jokes.
               (C) To indicate Mr. Wallace's
                    love of life.

(D) To show that non-fiction
is funnier than fiction.

The best answer to the question, "What is the speaker's probable purpose in mentioning humor in the *Digest*?" is (C), "To indicate Mr. Wallace's love of life." Therefore, you should choose answer (C).

36 (A) The same day.   (C) In two days.
    (B) The following day.   (D) The following week.

37 (A) On Thursday evening.   (C) On Saturday evening.
    (B) On Friday afternoon.   (D) On Sunday afternoon.

38 (A) Attending on the week end.   (C) Having the seats together.
    (B) Going in the afternoon.   (D) Sitting in the balcony.

39 (A) To make a reservation.   (C) To check a reservation.
    (B) To cancel a reservation.   (D) To change a reservation.

40 (A) Both of them.   (C) Only the first.
    (B) Neither of them.   (D) Only the second.

41 (A) Problems with aircraft.   (C) Too many passengers.
    (B) Problems with computers.   (D) Too few pilots and passengers.

42 (A) By calling her back.   (C) By rewriting her ticket.
    (B) By making her reservation.   (D) By meeting her at the airport.

43 (A) As money.   (C) As land.
    (B) As houses.   (D) As gold and silver.

44 (A) They have no effect on it.
    (B) They help promote it slightly.
    (C) They help promote it greatly.
    (D) They tend generally to limit it.

45 (A) Bank savings.   (C) Population.
    (B) Productive investment.   (D) Property purchases.

46 (A) Precious metals.   (C) Government policies.
    (B) Population pressures.   (D) Agricultural practices.

47 (A) To come for supper.   (C) To ask for help.
    (B) To invite him for supper.   (D) To see if he is well.

48 (A) Have supper at the man's place.
    (B) Take her daughter to the doctor.
    (C) Prepare supper for her family.
    (D) Change her baby's diaper.

Practice Test IV

49 (A) Bathing. (C) Eating.
   (B) Sleeping. (D) Playing.

50 (A) Happy to assist the woman. (C) Worried about his children.
   (B) Annoyed for being disturbed. (D) Grateful for the woman's help.

THIS IS THE END OF THE LISTENING COMPREHENSION PORTION OF THE TEST. LOOK AT THE TIME NOW, BEFORE YOU BEGIN WORK ON SECTION 2. USE *EXACTLY 25 MINUTES* TO WORK ON SECTION 2.

Section 2
Structure and Written Expression

Time: 25 minutes

This section is designed to measure your ability to recognize language that is appropriate for standard written English. There are two types of questions in this section, with special directions for each type.

Part A

Directions: Questions 1–15 are incomplete sentences. Four words or phrases, marked (A), (B), (C), (D), are given beneath the sentence. You are to choose the one word or phrase that best completes the sentence. Then, on your answer sheet, find the number of the problem and mark your answer.

Example I.   Sample Answer

We got a lot of exercise during our holiday in   (A) ● (C) (D)
the Swiss Alps ----- skiing every day.

(A) to
(B) by
(C) in
(D) on

In English, the sentence should read, "We got a lot of exercise during our holiday in the Swiss Alps by skiing every day." Therefore, you should choose (B).

Example II.   Sample Answer

Los Angeles never gets snowstorms and   (A) (B) (C) ●
Honolulu -----.

(A) is too.
(B) does too.
(C) isn't either.
(D) doesn't either.

The sentence should read, "Los Angeles never gets snowstorms and Honolulu doesn't either." Therefore, you should choose (D).

As soon as you understand the directions, begin work on the problems.

1 While determining the cause of a serious illness, -----.

   (A) the patient should be given good care by the doctor
   (B) the illness should be treated at once by the doctor

89

Practice Test IV

(C) the doctor should be giving the patient good care
(D) the most effective treatment should be employed by the doctor

2 The government asked the people to be sure to avoid ----- any water which had not been boiled.

(A) drinking
(B) to drink
(C) having drunk
(D) not to be drunk

3 No one was sure ----- Ron would come to the party or not.

(A) why
(B) when
(C) whether
(D) what time

4 The kilometer is ----- as the mile.

(A) less short
(B) the lesser length
(C) not as long
(D) much shorter

5 To reach the corner of 4th and Davison most directly from here, ----- straight ahead for about two miles, before turning left at the fifth traffic light and then going on for two more blocks.

(A) drive
(B) you're driving
(C) to drive
(D) you go driving

6 Before his death last year, Professor Talline decided that he ----- leave $200,000 to his university.

(A) can   (B) would   (C) may   (D) shall

7 Was Columbus the first man ----- the New World?

(A) discover
(B) discovered
(C) to discover
(D) who discovers

8 As you pass the courthouse, you'll be able to see Mr. Watson's orange groves -----.

(A) on your right
(B) to your right side
(C) on your right hand
(D) to your right-handed side

9 It's true that the old road is less direct and so a bit longer. We don't take the new one, -----, because we don't feel as safe on it.

(A) anyway
(B) though
(C) therefore
(D) otherwise

10 -----, Shirley thought Bill was Carol's husband but later she realized he wasn't.

(A) First
(B) At first
(C) Firstly
(D) First of all

Structure and Written Expression

11 This was once a very prosperous part of the city, but now many of the businesses have moved away or gone -----.

   (A) bankrupt
   (B) bankruptcy
   (C) bankrupted
   (D) to bankruptcy

12 Mr. Trane preferred to name the new baby Thomas but his wife said she wanted to call -----.

   (A) George
   (B) him George
   (C) he is George
   (D) George to him

13 ----- about the tragedy, we would never have come without first calling.

   (A) If we hear
   (B) If we heard
   (C) Did we hear
   (D) Had we heard

14 Some of the milk turned sour before reaching the market and ----- away.

   (A) must throw
   (B) had to throw
   (C) must be thrown
   (D) had to be thrown

15 The sign on the lawn says clearly that people ----- not walk on the grass.

   (A) will
   (B) might
   (C) have
   (D) may

Part B

Directions: In questions 16–40 each sentence has four words or phrases underlined. The four underlined parts of the sentence are marked (A), (B), (C), (D). You are to identify the one underlined word or phrase that should be corrected or rewritten. Then on your answer sheet, find the number of the problem and mark your answer.

Example I.   Sample Answer

One of Mrs. Wilson's <u>daughters</u> <u>doesn't play</u>   Ⓐ Ⓑ ● Ⓓ
                         A   B
the piano as <u>skillful</u> as the other one <u>does</u>.
                C   D

Answer (C), the underlined adjective skillful, would not be accepted in carefully written English. The adverb skillfully should be used instead. Therefore, the sentence should read: "One of Mrs. Wilson's daughters doesn't play the piano as skillfully as the other one does." To answer the problem correctly, you would choose (C).

91

Practice Test IV

Example II.

The woman <u>said</u> she <u>had saw</u> the robbery
          A   B

<u>take place</u> <u>on</u> the previous day.
   C   D

Sample Answer

(A) ● (C) (D)

Answer (B), the underlined phrase <u>had saw</u>, should not be used in carefully written English. The form <u>seen</u> should be used after <u>had</u>. Therefore, the sentence should read, "The woman said she had seen the robbery take place on the previous day." To answer the problem correctly, you would choose (B).

As soon as you understand the directions, begin work on the problems.

16 The most <u>powerful</u> countries <u>tend</u> to have the greatest <u>influential</u> <u>on</u>
                  A   B   C   D
    world affairs.

17 The <u>young ladies</u> in the Miss Universe contest must <u>not only</u> look
             A   B
    <u>beautifully</u> but demonstrate some <u>artistic</u> ability.
        C   D

18 Vatican City and the Coliseum <u>are</u> among the most <u>famous sights</u> which
                                        A   B
    visitors can see <u>them</u> <u>in</u> Rome.
                    C   D

19 <u>Technically</u> speaking, astronauts <u>can be able</u> to <u>visit the</u> moon and live
        A   B   C
    there <u>briefly</u>.
            D

20 While the space ship <u>had been</u> readied for launching, <u>its</u> pilots continued
                             A   B
    <u>watching</u> their instrument panel, to be sure everything was <u>all right</u>.
      C   D

21 The <u>elephant</u> is often described <u>that it is</u> the largest of <u>all</u> <u>land animals</u>.
            A   B   C   D

22 Fish can, <u>of course</u>, be <u>frozen</u> but in some societies people will eat
                A   B
    seafood <u>only</u> if it always tastes <u>freshly</u>.
            C   D

Structure and Written Expression

23 Without its thick fur, polar bears would quickly freeze to death in the icy
          A   B   C   D
northern waters.

24 In organic farming, the farmers avoid to use pesticides and chemical
   A   B   C   D
fertilizers.

25 The concrete is a building material made by mixing cement and sand
   A   B
with gravel and water.
 C   D

26 A friend of mine has been to that country three times, in spite most
        A   B   C
outsiders still can't get in.
                   D

27 While researchers cannot prove with complete certainty that smoking
                                            A
causes cancer, they theorize, therefore, that there is a very strong link
  B   C
between them.
   D

28 Between five and ten percentage of Europe's workers have been affected
                      A   B   C
by unemployment in recent years.
                        D

29 Several doctors in the area was asked to form a new regional medical
         A   B   C   D
association.

30 Lately, Don has been tired very much, so his friend said he should relax
   A   B   C
for a few days.
   D

31 It is much easier for a foreigner to become an American citizen if he has
     A   B   C
a close relative whoever is already an American.
               D

32 The painter Gauguin went to the South Pacific islands to paint in there.
   A   B   C   D

Practice Test IV

33 When a passenger gets on an American taxi, the driver sets the meter so
       A   B   C
    bargaining is avoided.
        D

34 Supercomputers are very useful in prediction the weather.
             A   B   C   D

35 Parents realize they need to teach their young children to cross a street
             A   B   C
    very careful.
      D

36 We can look forward for many more exciting scientific advances by
                    A   B   C
    the year 2000.
      D

37 The majority of countries are very concerned that if whaling does not
         A   B
    stop, or else nearly all the whales will disappear.
       C   D

38 Dr. Edwards has repeatedly advised patients to stop to smoke, if they
                A   B
    hope to stay in good health.
     C   D

39 The World Health Organization has done much to try to create a more
                                    A   B   C
    healthiest world.
       D

40 The technological progress of this last few decades has been truly
                   A   B   C
    amazing.
      D

DO NOT WORK ON ANY OTHER SECTION OF THE TEST

IF YOU FINISH IN LESS THAN 25 MINUTES,
CHECK YOUR WORK ON SECTION 2 ONLY. AT THE
END OF 25 MINUTES, GO ON TO SECTION 3.
USE *EXACTLY 45 MINUTES* TO WORK ON SECTION 3.

Section 3
Reading Comprehension and Vocabulary

Time: 45 minutes

There are two types of questions in this section, with special directions for each type.

Part A

Directions: In questions 1–30 each sentence has a word or phrase underlined. Below each sentence are four other words or phrases. You are to choose the one word or phrase which would best keep the meaning of the original sentence if it were substituted for the underlined word or phrase. Look at the example.

Example.   Sample Answer

The lecture hall is practically full now.   Ⓐ Ⓑ ● Ⓓ

  (A) half   (C) almost
  (B) hardly   (D) completely

The best answer is (C), because the sentence, "The lecture hall is almost full now," is closest in meaning to the original sentence, "The lecture hall is practically full now." Therefore, you should mark answer (C).

As soon as you understand the directions, begin work on the problems.

1 The Johnsons may decide to curtail their visit to Hawaii.

   (A) cancel   (C) lengthen
   (B) shorten   (D) re-schedule

2 It was realized later that a serious nuclear accident had just been averted.

   (A) avowed   (C) avoided
   (B) averred   (D) avenged

3 The building was evacuated within a very short time.

   (A) opened   (C) cleaned
   (B) emptied   (D) painted

95

Reading Comprehension and Vocabulary

4 These chemicals have been found to be toxic to human life.

   (A) useful   (C) essential
   (B) harmless   (D) poisonous

5 The teacher said that Alice did not conduct herself as she might have done.

   (A) enjoy   (C) explain
   (B) behave   (D) introduce

6 Mr. Smith inadvertently revealed to us a business secret.

   (A) obviously   (C) unintentionally
   (B) surprisingly   (D) unquestionably

7 The army returned from its battle triumphantly.

   (A) bravely   (C) exhaustively
   (B) belatedly   (D) victoriously

8 The troops must be disciplined when necessary.

   (A) rewarded   (C) recruited
   (B) punished   (D) discharged

9 My brother notified the neighbors last night, I believe.

   (A) visited   (C) assisted
   (B) noticed   (D) informed

10 I hope Dave will finally make up his mind.

   (A) decide   (C) get well
   (B) arrive   (D) wake up

11 That tank of water is portable.

   (A) made of steel   (C) easy to move
   (B) safe to drink   (D) connected to pipes

12 The composer of this piece of music was anonymous.

   (A) died young   (C) used a pen name
   (B) was unknown   (D) wrote only folk songs

13 Mr. Smalley's attempt to get the information was in vain.

   (A) distasteful   (C) unacceptable
   (B) unsuccessful   (D) incomparable

14 Mr. Jackson is considered a man of moderate views.

  (A) modern   (C) reasonable
  (B) stern   (D) predictable

15 Priscilla's contract cannot be terminated for five years.

  (A) ended   (C) renewed
  (B) changed   (D) publicized

16 The company asked for an assessment of the student.

  (A) an expression   (C) an evaluation
  (B) a transcript   (D) a recommendation

17 It is characteristic of that bird to sing every morning at dawn.

  (A) typical   (C) charming
  (B) cunning   (D) thoughtful

18 I have heard that those men are now under surveillance.

  (A) being watched   (C) mapping property
  (B) being questioned (D) working underground

19 Those clothes will be inappropriate for this evening.

  (A) unsuitable   (C) unavailable
  (B) unbearable   (D) unattractive

20 The main topic of discussion was Dr. Soames' objectionable comments.

  (A) relevant   (C) purposeful
  (B) offensive   (D) unprejudiced

21 The 1920s were a time of great transition.

  (A) change   (C) excitement
  (B) travel   (D) opportunity

22 That group was excellent at handling clandestine operations.

  (A) secret   (C) cautious
  (B) medical   (D) difficult

23 A new law was passed to obtain more revenue for the local government.

  (A) money   (C) offices
  (B) power   (D) employees

Reading Comprehension and Vocabulary

24 Many European cities are famous for their <u>cathedrals</u>.

    (A) great churches   (C) excellent museums
    (B) fine restaurants   (D) ancient traditions

25 The children <u>are susceptible to</u> flu at this time of year.

    (A) get shots for   (C) dress warmly to prevent
    (B) are likely to get   (D) are healthy enough to avoid

26 Would you please <u>elaborate on</u> your first point?

    (A) indicate   (C) begin the discussion on
    (B) write down   (D) give more information about

27 Smith expects his children to be <u>inquisitive</u>.

    (A) healthy   (C) curious
    (B) naughty   (D) serious

28 No one will <u>put up with</u> Dan's behaviour any more.

    (A) praise   (C) tolerate
    (B) criticize   (D) encourage

29 Marie seemed to be quite <u>nonchalant about</u> the trouble down the street.

    (A) excited by   (C) frightened of
    (B) unaware of   (D) unconcerned by

30 Most of the conversation between the two men was <u>intelligible</u>.

    (A) rapid   (C) disagreeable
    (B) clever   (D) understandable

Part B

<u>Directions</u>: The remaining questions in this section are based on a variety of reading material (single sentences, paragraphs, advertisements, and the like). In questions 31–60, you are to choose the <u>one</u> best answer, (A), (B), (C), or (D), to each question. Then on your answer sheet, find the number of the problem and mark your answer. Answer all questions following a passage on the basis of what is <u>stated</u> or <u>implied</u> in that passage.

    Read the following sample passage.

    Normally, the human body combats an infection by producing antibodies to the invading disease. These seek out the intruder and destroy it. These antibodies persist in the bloodstream for long periods and prevent reinfection.

Example I.

The passage says that the main function of antibodies is to

(A) attack the human body.
(B) invade other organisms.
(C) produce other antibodies.
(D) fight invading diseases.

Sample Answer
(A) (B) (C) ●

The passage says that the body fights (combats) disease by producing antibodies. Therefore, you should choose answer (D).

Example II:

The article says that, after an infection from a particular disease has been cured, the antibodies

(A) all disappear.
(B) continue to increase.
(C) remain in the blood.
(D) gradually decline in number.

Sample Answer
(A) (B) ● (D)

The passage says that the antibodies remain (persist) in the blood for a long time and prevent the disease from recurring. Therefore, you should choose (C) as the best completion of the sentence. Now continue.

As soon as you understand the directions, begin work on the problems.

Questions 31–33

Ice can literally electrify a thunderstorm. When big hailstones collide with tiny ice crystals, they seem to knock off one electric charge from the crystal. The stone gets a negative charge and the crystal becomes positive. As the heavy stones fall to earth and the tiny crystals waft up warm air currents, the separation of charges creates an unstable column of air. It releases its energy as a giant spark – lightning.

31 The main idea of this paragraph about storms is to explain

   (A) why big hailstones fall.
   (B) how lightning is created.
   (C) why warm air currents occur.
   (D) how ice crystals are formed.

32 According to the passage, changes in the electrical charges of particles in the storm are caused by

   (A) chemical reactions.
   (B) the rain falling from the sky.
   (C) collisions between the particles.
   (D) the mixing of warm and cold air currents.

Reading Comprehension and Vocabulary

33 The passage says that the principal reason why the hailstones and ice crystals move in different directions is that they have very different

(A) weights.
(B) charges.
(C) temperatures.
(D) shapes.

Questions 34–39

The British ship H.M.S Breadalbane sank in the Canadian Arctic on August 21, 1853, after being crushed by encroaching ice while on a rescue mission. The 21 crewmen aboard escaped over the ice to a companion vessel as the Breadalbane went down in 15 minutes.

Canadian scientists now report that after a three-year search of records about the ship, they have located it sitting upright in 110 meters of water. Using a robot camera device, they said they have taken remarkably clear pictures of the Breadalbane, which has been well preserved by the ice and the supercold water. "What we have is a treasure trove of 19th century Arctic exploration," reported one scientist. Located 1000 kilometers above the Arctic Circle, the Breadalbane is the world's northernmost known shipwreck.

34 According to the passage, the Breadalbane was sailing where it was on August 21, 1853, mainly to

(A) explore the area in which it sank.
(B) defend that area for the British government.
(C) find a northwest passage to the Orient.
(D) save the lives of other people.

35 What happened to the Breadalbane's crew?

(A) Some survived but most perished.
(B) Most survived but a few perished.
(C) All perished in the accident.
(D) All were rescued by another ship.

36 The scientists can prove they have found the exact location of the Breadalbane because they

(A) have taken underwater photos of the ship.
(B) dived down to the wreck to explore it.
(C) managed to refloat the boat using modern engineering techniques.
(D) retrieved some objects from the wreck with the ship's name on them.

37 The reason that the scientists called the wreck a "treasure trove" is that they expect it to yield a lot of

(A) precious metals.
(B) valuable foreign goods.
(C) precious stones.
(D) valuable information.

38 The main reason that they can be sure to expect to learn a great deal about 19th century Arctic exploration from the wreck is that

(A) no other ship ever sank in waters so far north.
(B) water currents are gentle there so the ship was not moved.
(C) the camera they are using is a robot.
(D) the ship has been extremely well preserved by the severe cold.

39 The principal historical distinction of this wreck, when compared with others, is that

(A) it has lain undisturbed for so long.
(B) the scientists expect to become wealthy from its discovery.
(C) no other has ever been found so far north.
(D) until now it has been impossible to take pictures in such icy waters.

Questions 40–43

This container is pressurised. Keep away from heat including the sun. Do not puncture or incinerate. FLAMMABLE – do not use near fire or flame. Keep out of reach of young children.

40 The above note on the container described is intended to

(A) encourage customers to buy it.
(B) help users understand how to remove its contents.
(C) prevent small children from spilling its contents.
(D) give owners a warning against careless mishandling.

41 Most of the instructions emphasize the importance of keeping the container

(A) under high pressure.
(B) far from heat or fire.
(C) away from careless people.
(D) out of the hands of children.

42 Although the note does not say so, it can be assumed that the sun is mentioned because of the possible

(A) effect of the sun's bright warm light.
(B) danger of penetrating radiation.
(C) advantages of keeping the container outside rather than inside.
(D) need for good ventilation while using the product.

43 The reason the container advises against having it near a flame is probably to prevent it from

(A) exploding.
(B) being punctured.
(C) emptying too quickly.
(D) having its pressure reduced.

Reading Comprehension and Vocabulary

Questions 44–48

The information on a full printed page can quickly be sent great distances by means of a facsimile transmitter. A laser beam scans the original image. What it "sees" it translates either into a series of electronic impulses which travel down telephone wires or into radio waves which are reflected off satellites to a receiving station. There the data are decoded and fed to an electronic pen.

44 The information sent by this system is carried great distances

 (A) on a printed page. (C) on a beam of light.
 (B) as electric pulses. (D) as sound waves.

45 The "original image" (sentence 2) is the same as the

 (A) printed page. (C) laser beam.
 (B) transmitter. (D) receiving station.

46 When does the laser beam come into operation?

 (A) Before the message is sent.
 (B) After the message has been transmitted.
 (C) Before the message is first printed.
 (D) After the message is decoded.

47 The final step in the transmission process described certainly must be

 (A) receiving the information at the receiving station.
 (B) decoding the electronic impulses.
 (C) printing the information on a new page of paper.
 (D) bouncing the message off of a satellite.

48 A major advantage of this system, according to the passage, is its

 (A) cost. (C) novelty.
 (B) speed. (D) accuracy.

Questions 49–53

Seventy per cent of all living species including all dinosaurs were wiped off the surface of the earth 65 million years ago. There have been various theories that their extinction was caused by a great catastrophe of one sort or another. But now, instead of mere speculation, it has almost become an established fact that a meteor did the job.

The impact on earth of a large meteorite would have raised a dust veil blocking off enough sunlight to stop photosynthesis, the process by which plants make the food necessary for their survival. This would have killed them, destroying the food on which animals depended, and would have triggered a brief Ice Age, reducing still further the number of survivors.

Practice Test IV

49 The writer states as a fact that about 65 million years ago, most species of plants and animals

   (A) migrated from the land into the water.
   (B) moved to the surface of the earth.
   (C) were destroyed completely.
   (D) had not yet been created.

50 The passage states that it is most likely that the extinction of many species was caused by

   (A) an object from outer space.
   (B) a nuclear explosion on earth.
   (C) a large increase in global temperature.
   (D) intense radiation from outer space.

51 According to the article, which one of the following effects of the collision would have been most harmful to plants?

   (A) The great heat.   (C) A severe earthquake.
   (B) Dangerous radiation.   (D) Dark clouds covering the sun.

52 As a result of the impact upon plantlife, the passage implies that animals would probably have

   (A) temporarily stopped having young.
   (B) eventually starved to death.
   (C) greatly changed their diets.
   (D) rapidly moved to other places.

53 In addition to stopping photosynthesis, the dust veil caused

   (A) blindness in surviving animals.
   (B) widespread outbreaks of illness.
   (C) very low temperatures worldwide.
   (D) a slight increase in plant species.

Questions 54–58

In recent years, scientists have developed a number of techniques in genetic engineering. Most aim at modifying the hereditary mechanisms of micro-organisms or cells for purposes of research or commerce. Others include the fusion of cells, DNA synthesis, and the creation of hybridomas, long-lived cells that are designed to produce pure antibodies for use against disease. But of all these marvels, it is gene splicing that scientists consider the most exciting. Says the University of Zurich's Charles Weissman, 50, who in 1980 became the first scientist to make bacteria produce a facsimile of human interferon (a possible weapon with which to attack cancer): "Biology has become as unthinkable without gene-splicing techniques as sending an explorer into the jungle without a compass."

Reading Comprehension and Vocabulary

54 Which one of the following techniques of genetic engineering is employed to modify the mechanisms of heredity in an organism?

(A) The creation of hybridomas. (C) Gene splicing.
(B) Cell fusion. (D) DNA synthesis.

55 Antibodies against disease can apparently be produced in the laboratory from

(A) hybridomas. (C) spliced genes.
(B) fused cells. (D) artificially synthesized DNA.

56 According to the passage, the technique that interests genetic engineers the most is

(A) producing interferon. (C) cell fusion.
(B) gene splicing. (D) creating hybridomas.

57 The interferon that Professor Weissman produced was notable for being the first

(A) ever to have been created.
(B) to successfully cure cancer.
(C) ever to be located and identified in a human being.
(D) ever to be synthesized in a laboratory.

58 The quotation of Professor Weissman is basically intended to explain that

(A) interferon is as vital to biology as a compass is to a jungle.
(B) the jungle is as important to an explorer as biology is to genetic engineering.
(C) an explorer should not enter the jungle without a compass.
(D) gene splicing henceforth will be a fundamental part of biology.

Questions 59–60

For each of these questions, choose the answer that is <u>closest in meaning</u> to the original sentence. Note that several of the choices may be factually correct, but you should choose the one that is the <u>closest restatement of the given sentence.</u>

59 Allwright certainly got what was coming to him.

(A) Allwright definitely deserved his punishment.
(B) Allwright surely obtained his package on time.
(C) Allwright definitely received his gift promptly.
(D) Allwright was surely informed of everything he needed to know.

60 For a student, Joe seemed to spend a surprising amount of time doing nothing.
  (A) Joe seemed surprised to find his student friend wasting time.
  (B) Joe didn't seem to be doing anything when a friend surprised him at school.
  (C) Joe seemed to do nothing for his friends while he was a student.
  (D) Joe seemed to have a lot of free time despite being a student.

DO NOT WORK ON ANY OTHER SECTION OF THE TEST.

IF YOU FINISH IN LESS THAN 45 MINUTES, CHECK YOUR WORK ON SECTION 3 ONLY. AT THE END OF 45 MINUTES STOP WORK AND CLOSE YOUR TEST BOOK.

Tapescript

Practice Tests I through IV

Before you begin any of these tests, remove the answer sheets from the back of the book.

When you take the actual TOEFL, you will have only a pencil, an eraser, your watch and the test book and answer sheet on your desk. You will not be allowed to take any dictionaries or other books into the test room.

You must not write in the test book – mark all your answers clearly on the answer sheet provided by completely blackening the oval which corresponds to the answer you have chosen. If you wish to change an answer, completely erase your first answer and mark your new answer.

Answer every question – mark your best guess if you are not sure of an answer.

Practice Test I

Print your name in the box provided at the top of the answer sheet. Print your family name (or surname) first. Then print your first name. You will now have 15 seconds to do this.

[15 second pause]

Now open your book at Practice Test I and listen to the directions for the Listening Comprehension Section:

Tapescript

Practice Test I
Section 1
Listening Comprehension

In this section of the test, you will have an opportunity to demonstrate your ability to understand spoken English. There are three parts to this section, with special directions for each part.

Part A

Directions: For each problem in Part A, you will hear a short statement. The statements will be spoken just one time. They will not be written out for you, and you must listen carefully in order to understand what the speaker says.

When you hear a statement, read the four sentences in your test book and decide which one is closest in meaning to the statement you have heard. Then, on your answer sheet, find the number of the problem and mark your answer.

Listen to the following example:

You will hear: Unlike her brother, Anne usually prefers a small breakfast.

You will read: (A) Anne doesn't like her brother.
(B) Anne usually eats no breakfast.
(C) Anne eats a smaller breakfast than her brother.
(D) Anne's brother eats as much as she does for breakfast.

Sentence (C), "Anne eats a smaller breakfast than her brother," means most nearly the same as the statement: "Unlike her brother, Anne usually prefers a small breakfast." Therefore, you should choose answer (C).

Listen to the next example:

You will hear: Mrs. Weller has on a fortune in jewelry.

You will read: (A) Mrs. Weller owns a lot of expensive jewelry.
(B) Mrs. Weller is wearing a lot of expensive jewelry today.
(C) Mrs. Weller is lucky to be married to such a wealthy man.
(D) Mrs. Weller's family owns the biggest jewelry store in town.

Sentence (B), "Mrs. Weller is wearing a lot of expensive jewelry today," is closest in meaning to the sentence: "Mrs. Weller has on a fortune in jewelry." Therefore, you should choose answer (B).

Practice Test I

Now let us begin Part A with question number 1.

1. The members of the audience gave the orchestra a big hand.
2. Marvin worked his way through the first four years of college.
3. If Janet had checked her purse, she wouldn't have forgotten her license at home.
4. Laura had the TV on when her parents entered the room.
5. There's never a parking problem at this shopping center.
6. Nothing anyone said seemed to influence Jack's views very much.
7. To be quite honest, I can't stand the taste of cigarettes.
8. The vet showed Tom how to mix the medicine into the cattle feed.
9. Bill sleeps more soundly than anyone else I have ever known.
10. Mrs. Carson reminded her daughters of their table manners.
11. Jeff couldn't figure out what was the matter with Carol.
12. The Landons doubted if it was worth driving a hundred miles to see the basketball game.
13. On this bus route, passengers put the exact change in the box for their tickets, since the driver doesn't handle any cash.
14. Margaret changed her mind about going to Paris and had her ticket refunded.
15. The editor fired Ted for a careless disregard of the facts.
16. The bill already includes a service charge, so don't leave over 10 per cent.
17. Mrs. Douglas unknowingly left a package lying on the shop counter.
18. Betty says that on a day like this, it's really good to be warm and comfortable inside.
19. The lady informed me that tickets for this evening's concert are sold out.
20. You may have heard the news that Mr. and Mrs. Collins are now separated.

This is the end of Part A.

Now listen to the directions for Part B, as they are read to you.

Part B

<u>Directions</u>: In Part B you will hear fifteen short conversations between

Tapescript

two speakers. At the end of each conversation, a third voice will ask a question about what was said. The question will be spoken just one time. After you hear a conversation and the question about it, read the four possible answers and decide which one would be the best answer to the question you have heard. Then, on your answer sheet, find the number of the problem and mark your answer.

Listen to the following example:

You will hear:

WOMAN:	What plans have you made for your summer vacation?
MAN:	Hiking with friends in the Himalayas. We leave in mid-June and return at the end of August.
QUESTION:	How long will the man be gone?

You will read: (A) A month.
(B) 1½ months.
(C) Two months.
(D) 2½ months.

From the conversation, we know that the friends will leave in mid-June and return in late August. The best answer, then, is (D), "2½ months." Therefore you should choose answer (D).

Now let us begin Part B with question number 21.

21 WOMAN: Did you hear Mike is in the hospital with head injuries and a broken arm?
   MAN: Yes. Apparently he was struck by another vehicle and turned completely over.
   QUESTION: What happened to Mike?

22 MAN: We had better hurry or we'll miss part of the show.
   WOMAN: The previews last around 20 minutes, so we should still get there in time.
   QUESTION: Where are the man and woman going?

23 WOMAN: Hi, Bob. Come on in. I'm glad you could make it to the party this evening. But where's Jane?
   MAN: She sends her apologies. She has a big exam tomorrow and wants to be sure she's ready for it.
   QUESTION: What's Jane doing this evening?

24 WOMAN: How can the new students find out about social events on campus?
   MAN: All they have to do is get the campus paper each day and check the social calendar.

Practice Test I

	QUESTION:	How does the man suggest new students learn about campus social activities?
25	MAN:	There's really nothing of value in this envelope, but the documents inside must not be lost.
	WOMAN:	Then, to be on the safe side, you ought to send it registered, I think.
	QUESTION:	How does the woman think the letter should be sent?
26	WOMAN:	Three days of taking medication for this cold hasn't resulted in any improvement at all.
	MAN:	We always think we should take something. But whether it does any good is another matter.
	QUESTION:	How does the man feel about taking medication for a cold?
27	WOMAN:	I just heard the bad news about your job.
	MAN:	Well, the company is automating the office, so a lot of people are being let go.
	QUESTION:	What happened to the man?
28	MAN:	No doubt you have already heard of the passing of Mrs. Whitworth.
	WOMAN:	Yes, services will be held for her tomorrow at St. Luke's Church.
	QUESTION:	What is known about Mrs. Whitworth?
29	WOMAN:	How much do you pay for this magazine at the newsstand?
	MAN:	I don't know because I subscribe. Although it comes a few days later, it costs about 45 per cent less overall.
	QUESTION:	What is the man's reason for subscribing to the magazine?
30	WOMAN:	I do hope Peter does well in his studies this semester.
	MAN:	When our son promises to get good marks, you can count on him.
	QUESTION:	What kind of student does the man consider his son?
31	WOMAN:	Your wife says you were stopped today for speeding and got a ticket.
	MAN:	That's right. The patrolman was going to let me off with just a warning until I couldn't find my license.
	QUESTION:	What did the man receive from the patrolman?

Tapescript

32 WOMAN: That's a shame about your motorcycle being stolen yesterday.
   MAN: I'd had it only five months and hadn't even finished paying for it.
   QUESTION: What is known about the man's purchase of the motorcycle?

33 MAN: How did you like the movie last night?
   WOMAN: Considering the reviews it had received, we were expecting a much better film.
   QUESTION: How did the woman feel about the movie?

34 MAN: The city council has finally voted the funds to build a new high school.
   WOMAN: It's about time! I don't know what took them so long!
   QUESTION: What's the woman's opinion about the school?

35 MAN: To teach those students English, do you have to speak their language quite well?
   WOMAN: Quite the contrary. They benefit most when the class is conducted entirely in the foreign language.
   QUESTION: Which language is used in the woman's classes?

This is the end of Part B.

Now look at the directions for Part C, as they are read to you.

Part C

Directions: In this part of the test, you will hear several short talks and/or conversations. After each talk or conversation, you will be asked some questions. The talks and questions will be spoken just one time. They will not be written out for you, so you will have to listen carefully in order to understand and remember what the speaker says.

When you hear a question, read the four possible answers in your test book and decide which one would be the best answer to the question you have heard. Then, on your answer sheet, find the number of the problem and fill in (blacken) the space that corresponds to the letter of the answer you have chosen.

Listen to this sample talk:

DeWitt Wallace founded the *Reader's Digest* as a pocket-sized, non-fiction magazine intended to inform, enlighten and entertain. He wanted to condense in the *Digest* the best of previously published material. He filled the magazine with articles that celebrated the values

Practice Test I

he most admired in his nation: hard work, thrift, a calm courage through difficult times, love of God, family and country, and laughter – much laughter.

The first issue in February 1922 had a print order of only 5000 copies. When DeWitt Wallace passed away in June 1981, the *Reader's Digest* had become the world's most widely read magazine, with an estimated 100 million readers each month, and was published in 16 languages.

Now listen to the first question on the sample talk:

You will hear: What kind of articles did Mr. Wallace mainly select for his magazine?

You will read: (A) Those emphasizing the profit motive.
(B) Those reflecting social values he admired.
(C) Those promoting his religious views.
(D) Those written by the best fiction writers.

The best answer to the question, "What kind of articles did Mr. Wallace mainly select for his magazine?" is (B), "Those reflecting social values he admired." Therefore, you should choose answer (B).

Now listen to the second question on the sample talk:

You will hear: What is the speaker's probable purpose in mentioning humor in the *Digest*?

You will read: (A) To stress the magazine's lack of seriousness.
(B) To teach readers many new jokes.
(C) To indicate Mr. Wallace's love of life.
(D) To show that non-fiction is funnier than fiction.

The best answer to the question, "What is the speaker's probable purpose in mentioning humor in the *Digest*?" is (C), "To indicate Mr. Wallace's love of life." Therefore, you should choose answer (C).

Questions 36 through 39 are based on the following telephone conversation.

MAN: Hello.
WOMAN: Hello. I noticed your want ad in the paper this morning.
MAN: You mean about my Mercedes 350?
WOMAN: That's right. I noticed it's a '79 and wondered about its condition.
MAN: Well, it's in great shape. I've been the only driver, and all maintenance has been done according to the dates specified in the service manual.
WOMAN: The ad said it has air conditioning, power brakes, power steering, automatic transmission and a convertible top.
MAN: That's right. I forgot to add that the tires and battery are all new, too. It has comprehensive insurance, with coverage for another eight months.
WOMAN: Do you mind my asking why you're selling the car?

Tapescript

MAN: Oh, my company is transferring me to Europe next month, so I plan to buy a new one over there.
WOMAN: I noticed you didn't mention any price in the ad.
MAN: We can negotiate that if you would like to come see it.
WOMAN: Fine. Where do you live?
MAN: At the corner of 8th and Parkhurst. I'll be home all evening. Come any time after 6:30.
WOMAN: All right. I'll be there around 7.

36 What does the man say is the condition of the car?
37 Why is the man selling the car?
38 After the conversation, what does the woman still not know?
39 When are the man and woman going to meet?

Questions 40 through 43 are based on the following conversation.

WOMAN: Good evening.
MAN: Hello. Do you have any vacancies here at your motel?
WOMAN: I believe there may be one. Did you make a reservation in advance?
MAN: No, we didn't.
WOMAN: Well, we just received word that one reservation has been canceled, so you arrived at a good time.
MAN: I suppose so. By the way, how much is the room?
WOMAN: It's $30, with color TV and an extra bedroom. We have a pool in the back.
MAN: That's good. We need the extra room with our two kids.
WOMAN: If this is agreeable, please step into our office to register.
MAN: Do you want the payment in advance?
WOMAN: That's our policy. I'm sure you understand.
MAN: Of course. What's the number of the unit?
WOMAN: No. 61, on the second floor, over on the right. Here's the key.
MAN: Thank you. I'll park the car over there first and get the family unloaded. Then I'll come right over to register.
WOMAN: Certainly, sir.

40 Why can the man and his family stay at this motel?
41 What is the man especially glad to have for his children?
42 When does the motel want its guests to pay?
43 What is the probable main reason for the motel's policy on payments?

Questions 44 through 46 are based on the following announcement.

Good afternoon. This is your captain speaking. We have been notified of the possibility of strong air turbulence ahead for the next forty miles or so. Passengers are therefore strongly advised to remain in their seats with

Practice Test I

their seat belts on for their own protection and to avoid use of the restrooms for the time being, if at all possible. During this time, young children should be firmly fastened into their seats.

Please observe these precautions until the seat-belt warning sign has gone off. Lunch will be served after we have passed through the air turbulence zone. Thank you.

44 Why has the captain asked passengers to keep their seat belts on?

45 What has the captain asked passengers not to do during this time?

46 When will the passengers be able to get up again?

Questions 47 through 50 are based on the following conversation.

MAN:	Good afternoon, Mrs. Keaton.
WOMAN:	Good afternoon, Mr. Duncan. Please come in and have a seat.
MAN:	Thank you.
WOMAN:	I have been looking through your application. You seem to have many of the qualifications needed for this position, especially experience.
MAN:	I have been in computer programming for eight years now.
WOMAN:	Yes, I see. Were you satisfied with your last position, Mr. Duncan?
MAN:	Generally, yes. But to be honest, not entirely. I was with a small, family-owned company, and chances for advancement were very limited.
WOMAN:	The letter of reference from the president praises your work highly.
MAN:	Mr. Darnton gave me a lot of responsibility and I learned a great deal about company operations.
WOMAN:	Well, we ask for loyalty and hard work from our employees. But we pay well, and opportunities for promotion depend on merit, not just age or seniority.
MAN:	I am very interested in working for your firm, Mrs. Keaton.
WOMAN:	I see. I have a few more applicants to interview today for this position. But at the moment, your chances look very good. We will be in touch with you shortly, Mr. Duncan.
MAN:	Thank you for your time, Mrs. Keaton. Good-bye.
WOMAN:	Good-bye.

47 Why has the man come to this office?

48 How did the man's firm regard him?

49 At the end of the conversation, how does the man probably feel?

50 What does the woman stress about her company's policies in giving promotions?

THIS IS THE END OF THE LISTENING
COMPREHENSION PORTION OF THE TEST.
LOOK AT THE TIME NOW, BEFORE YOU
BEGIN WORK ON SECTION 2. USE
EXACTLY 25 MINUTES TO WORK
ON SECTION 2.

Practice Test II

Print your name in the box provided at the top of the answer sheet. Print your family name (or surname) first. Then print your first name. You will now have 15 seconds to do this:

[15 second pause]

Now open your book at Practice Test II and listen to the directions for the Listening Comprehension Section:

Practice Test II
Section 1
Listening Comprehension

In this section of the test, you will have an opportunity to demonstrate your ability to understand spoken English. There are three parts to this section, with special directions for each part.

Part A

Directions: For each problem in Part A, you will hear a short statement. The statements will be spoken just one time. They will not be written out for you, and you must listen carefully in order to understand what the speaker says.

When you hear a statement, read the four sentences in your test book and decide which one is closest in meaning to the statement you have heard. Then, on your answer sheet, find the number of the problem and mark your answer.

    Listen to the following example:

    You will hear: Unlike her brother, Anne usually prefers a small breakfast.

    You will read: (A) Anne doesn't like her brother.
                        (B) Anne usually eats no breakfast.
                        (C) Anne eats a smaller breakfast than her brother.
                        (D) Anne's brother eats as much as she does for breakfast.

Tapescript

Sentence (C), "Anne eats a smaller breakfast than her brother," means most nearly the same as the statement: "Unlike her brother, Anne usually prefers a small breakfast." Therefore, you should choose answer (C).

Listen to the next example:

You will hear: Mrs. Weller has on a fortune in jewelry.

You will read: (A) Mrs. Weller owns a lot of expensive jewelry.
(B) Mrs. Weller is wearing a lot of expensive jewelry today.
(C) Mrs. Weller is lucky to be married to such a wealthy man.
(D) Mrs. Weller's family owns the biggest jewelry store in town.

Sentence (B), "Mrs. Weller is wearing a lot of expensive jewelry today," is closest in meaning to the sentence: "Mrs. Weller has on a fortune in jewelry." Therefore, you should choose answer (B).

Now let us begin Part A with question number 1.

1 The sisters looked forward to getting dresses for Christmas.
2 The forecast is for morning showers, light westerly winds and possibly some snow by noon.
3 The station has had so many requests for this song that we have decided to play the record over.
4 The doctor suggested how best to nurse Joe back to health.
5 The game ended up in a tie.
6 Mr. Wilson reminded his wife to water the lawn.
7 Linda seems to have very little regard for other people's feelings.
8 Officer Perkins said his men had found some clues at the scene of the crime.
9 John said he is likely to visit Yellowstone Park next summer for the first time.
10 Mr. Carter asked his wife if she would get his suit from the dry cleaners.
11 Sue goes to school at Columbia University.
12 Well, we'll be seeing you.
13 The next stop is the terminal for U.S. domestic carriers.
14 We hoped Rick would tell us what his new home was like.
15 The referee blew his whistle and brought the football game to a halt.
16 Nancy passed Ralph the meat and potatoes.

17 The firemen were in time to save the people but not the house.

18 With apples at 25 cents a pound, we couldn't resist taking four pounds.

19 The textbook has been selling rather slowly so the clerks still have plenty of copies left.

20 After getting on at the ground floor, John pushed button No. 5 and rode up five stories.

This is the end of Part A.

Now listen to the directions for Part B, as they are read to you.

Part B

Directions: In Part B you will hear fifteen short conversations between two speakers. At the end of each conversation, a third voice will ask a question about what was said. The question will be spoken just one time. After you hear a conversation and the question about it, read the four possible answers and decide which one would be the best answer to the question you have heard. Then, on your answer sheet, find the number of the problem and mark your answer.

Listen to the following example:

You will hear:

WOMAN:	What plans have you made for your summer vacation?
MAN:	Hiking with friends in the Himalayas. We leave in mid-June and return at the end of August.
QUESTION:	How long will the man be gone?

You will read: (A) A month.
(B) 1½ months.
(C) Two months.
(D) 2½ months.

From the conversation, we know that the friends will leave in mid-June and return in late August. The best answer, then, is (D), "2½ months." So you should choose answer (D).

Now, let us begin Part B with question number 21.

21	WOMAN:	These trousers turned out to be too small for my son, so I have brought them back for larger ones.
	MAN:	Certainly, madam. We can take them back if you have your receipt with you.
	QUESTION:	What does the woman wish to do?
22	MAN:	Excuse me. Did I leave my boarding pass here with you?

Tapescript

		Martin's the name.
	WOMAN:	Oh, yes, Mr. Martin. You left it lying here. There you are. Have a nice flight, sir.
	QUESTION:	What was the woman doing when she said: "There you are."?
23	MAN:	Let's see. I have printed my family name, middle name, first name, birthdate and address. Anything else?
	WOMAN:	No, that's fine. We'll fill in the rest if you'll just sign at the bottom.
	QUESTION:	What has the man been doing?
24	MAN:	Most foreign students here are graduate students in accounting, dentistry, engineering and business administration.
	WOMAN:	Right. They tend to major in practical fields that will assure them of good jobs later.
	QUESTION:	What does the woman believe foreign students consider important in choosing a major?
25	MAN:	I would like to cash this check for $20. Small bills, please.
	WOMAN:	Certainly, sir. Here you are: three fives and five ones.
	QUESTION:	How many bills did the customer receive?
26	MAN:	I can't find my lunch box anywhere. I know I had it when I arrived.
	WOMAN:	Never mind. I will treat you today at that cafe across the street.
	QUESTION:	What has the woman offered to do?
27	MAN:	The latest word is that this car factory will soon be shut down.
	WOMAN:	I'm not surprised. It just can't compete with more up-to-date plants.
	QUESTION:	Why is the factory being closed down?
28	MAN:	Good afternoon. I'm Mr. Jackson. I answered your ad for an experienced advertising executive.
	WOMAN:	Oh, yes, Mr. Jackson. Won't you have a seat. The manager will see you shortly.
	QUESTION:	Why is Mr. Jackson in that office?
29	WOMAN:	Why don't you and your family come for supper at our place this Saturday?
	MAN:	We would love to if we weren't already invited to my in-

Practice Test II

		laws that evening.
	QUESTION:	Where will the man and his family go on Saturday evening?
30	WOMAN:	I'm worried that man may soon run out of oil.
	MAN:	By then we will surely have cheap energy substitutes like power from the sun, the wind or the waves.
	QUESTION:	Why does the man mention other sources of energy?
31	WOMAN:	I was hoping to get some bread from the bakery before it closes.
	MAN:	My watch says 6:50, so we have around forty minutes left to get there.
	QUESTION:	What time does the bakery close?
32	MAN:	Is it true that the store replaced your dishwasher for nothing?
	WOMAN:	Yes, they had to because it was still on the warranty.
	QUESTION:	How much did the store charge for its service?
33	WOMAN:	With the company in such financial difficulties, I wonder what will happen to the president.
	MAN:	Haven't you heard? The board of directors has asked for his resignation.
	QUESTION:	What happened to the president of the company?
34	WOMAN:	Old Mrs. Harris is suing those people on the corner. Their children left some toys on the sidewalk and she fell in the dark and broke her leg.
	MAN:	Good. Mrs. Harris warned them about that before. Maybe a suit will make them more considerate.
	QUESTION:	What is Mrs. Harris going to do?
35	WOMAN:	What a remarkable performance the pianist gave this evening.
	MAN:	You could tell that the entire audience felt the same way.
	QUESTION:	How did the audience consider the performance?

This is the end of Part B.

Now look at the directions for Part C, as they are read to you.

Part C

Directions: In this part of the test, you will hear several short talks and/or conversations. After each talk or conversation, you will be asked some

Tapescript

questions. The talks and questions will be spoken just one time. They will not be written out for you, so you will have to listen carefully in order to understand and remember what the speaker says.

When you hear a question, read the four possible answers in your test book and decide which one would be the best answer to the question you have heard. Then, on your answer sheet, find the number of the problem and fill in (blacken) the space that corresponds to the letter of the answer you have chosen.

Listen to this sample talk:

DeWitt Wallace founded the *Reader's Digest* as a pocket-sized, non-fiction magazine intended to inform, enlighten and entertain. He wanted to condense in the *Digest* the best of previously published material. He filled the magazine with articles that celebrated the values he most admired in his nation: hard work, thrift, a calm courage through difficult times, love of God, family and country, and laughter – much laughter.

The first issue in February 1922 had a print order of only 5000 copies. When Dewitt Wallace passed away in June 1981, the *Reader's Digest* had become the world's most widely read magazine, with an estimated 100 million readers each month, and was published in 16 languages.

Now listen to the first question on the sample talk:

You will hear: What kind of articles did Mr. Wallace mainly select for his magazine?
You will read: (A) Those emphasizing the profit motive.
 (B) Those reflecting social values he admired.
 (C) Those promoting his religious views.
 (D) Those written by the best fiction writers.

The best answer to the question, "What kind of articles did Mr. Wallace mainly select for his magazine?" is (B), "Those reflecting social values he admired." Therefore, you should choose answer (B).

Now listen to the second question on the sample talk:

You will hear: What is the speaker's probable purpose in mentioning humor in the *Digest*?
You will read: (A) To stress the magazine's lack of seriousness.
 (B) To teach readers many new jokes.
 (C) To indicate Mr. Wallace's love of life.
 (D) To show that non-fiction is funnier than fiction.

The best answer to the question, "What is the speaker's probable purpose in mentioning humor in the *Digest*?" is (C), "To indicate Mr. Wallace's love of life." Therefore, you should choose answer (C).

Questions 36 through 39 are based on the following conversation.

MAN: Mrs. Spencer, what time is Mr. Tanaka's flight expected to

Practice Test II

	arrive at Kennedy Airport?
WOMAN:	Around 2 pm, sir. Will you go with the company car to meet him?
MAN:	Yes, so I'd better leave here no later than noon. How about the accommodations at the Hilton for Mr. Tanaka and his party?
WOMAN:	I made the reservations for them last week and checked again yesterday to be sure everything is ready.
MAN:	Including the banquet room for tonight's reception?
WOMAN:	That's right. The manager assured me that everything will be exactly as we have requested.
MAN:	Excellent. I want everything to be the very best.
WOMAN:	I'm sure it will be. That manager has never let us down yet.
MAN:	We want to make a good impression. Not just to be sure that this business deal is a success, but to pay back the wonderful hospitality we received from them in Tokyo last year.

36 What is the man going to do?

37 Where will Mr. Tanaka stay after his arrival?

38 What will take place that evening?

39 Why does the man want to make a good impression?

Questions 40 through 43 are based on the following conversation.

MAN:	Well, Mrs. King. How did you do on your driving test?
WOMAN:	Not so well, I'm afraid.
MAN:	Didn't you get your license?
WOMAN:	No. My score was only 57 per cent. The woman who tested me was very strict about everything.
MAN:	Where did you lose the most points?
WOMAN:	One thing was not turning my head before changing lanes or making turns.
MAN:	Right. Using a turn signal isn't enough. To be safe, you have to glance back over your shoulder in the direction you want to go.
WOMAN:	My teacher didn't emphasize that enough. Or about maintaining the right distance behind the car in front.
MAN:	That's right. You need a trailing distance of about one or two car lengths for every 10 miles per hour you're going.
WOMAN:	My parallel parking was good. I've been practicing that a lot.
MAN:	What was your worst moment?
WOMAN:	Waiting on an uphill slope for the light to change to green.
MAN:	What happened?
WOMAN:	Well, I let the car stall and forgot how to use the hand brake. So the car rolled back and bumped the one behind me.
MAN:	That alone probably failed you.

40 How did the woman do on her driving test?

41 What does the woman believe she did well?

Tapescript

42 What was the woman's problem when making a turn?

43 Why did the woman bump a car in traffic?

Questions 44 through 47 are based on the following weather report.

We interrupt this regularly scheduled program to bring you the following bulletin from the United States Weather Bureau. A severe weather alert is now in effect for all of southern Ohio and Indiana. A violent storm front is moving in a north-northeasterly direction. Severe thunderstorms with lightning and hail can be expected, with winds gusting to up to 90 miles per hour.

Stay tuned to this station for periodic bulletins from the weather bureau on the movement of this storm front, which may well produce scattered tornadoes. Sightings of tornadoes will be reported immediately. Remember to stay away from windows and to be ready to take shelter in your basement or in your storm shelter, if necessary. This severe weather alert will remain in effect at least until 10 p.m. tonight.

44 What is the main purpose of this announcement?

45 What is the general direction of the storm?

46 What are the announcer and listeners most concerned about in this weather bulletin?

47 During this storm, where is the best place to stay, according to the announcement?

Questions 48 through 50 are based on the following announcement.

This is a recorded announcement. Thank you for calling Gateway Booking, your one-stop center in Metropolitan New York for tickets for all professional sports. Our booking staff are presently engaged but will be with you shortly.

For your information, good seats are still available for Sunday's football game between the New York Giants and the Dallas Cowboys, and also for tomorrow's basketball game between the New York Knickerbockers and the Detroit Pistons. This evening's baseball playoff match between the New York Yankees and the Oakland Athletics has been canceled because of wet grounds and has been rescheduled for tomorrow afternoon.

48 To whom would this announcement be made?

49 Why is the announcement recorded?

50 Which sport has had a game in New York canceled?

THIS IS THE END OF THE LISTENING COMPREHENSION PORTION OF THE TEST. LOOK AT THE TIME NOW, BEFORE YOU BEGIN WORK ON SECTION 2. USE *EXACTLY 25 MINUTES* TO WORK ON SECTION 2.

Practice Test III

Print your name in the box provided at the top of the answer sheet. Print your family name (or surname) first. Then print your first name. You will now have 15 seconds to do this:

[15 second pause]

Now open your book at Practice Test III and listen to the directions for the Listening Comprehension Section:

Practice Test III
Section 1
Listening Comprehension

In this section of the test, you will have an opportunity to demonstrate your ability to understand spoken English. There are three parts to this section, with special directions for each part.

Part A

Directions: For each problem in Part A, you will hear a short statement. The statements will be spoken just one time. They will not be written out for you, and you must listen carefully in order to understand what the speaker says.

When you hear a statement, read the four sentences in your test book and decide which one is closest in meaning to the statement you have heard. Then, on your answer sheet, find the number of the problem and mark your answer.

Listen to the following example:

You will hear: Unlike her brother, Anne usually prefers a small breakfast.

You will read: (A) Anne doesn't like her brother.
(B) Anne usually eats no breakfast.
(C) Anne eats a smaller breakfast than her brother.
(D) Anne's brother eats as much as she does for breakfast.

Sentence (C), "Anne eats a smaller breakfast than her brother," means most nearly the same as the statement: "Unlike her brother, Anne usually prefers a small breakfast." Therefore, you should choose answer (C).

Tapescript

Listen to the next example:

You will hear: Mrs. Weller has on a fortune in jewelry.

You will read: (A) Mrs. Weller owns a lot of expensive jewelry.
(B) Mrs. Weller is wearing a lot of expensive jewelry today.
(C) Mrs. Weller is lucky to be married to such a wealthy man.
(D) Mrs. Weller's family owns the biggest jewelry store in town.

Sentence (B), "Mrs. Weller is wearing a lot of expensive jewelry today," is closest in meaning to the sentence: "Mrs. Weller has on a fortune in jewelry." Therefore, you should choose answer (B).

Now let us begin Part A with question number 1.

1. Mary says she would rather go to the clinic by herself.
2. During this spring sale, prices on all items have been reduced by up to one third.
3. Take Eighth Street to Main and you will see Lim's restaurant right on the corner opposite the bank.
4. My lighter seems to be out of fluid. Can I trouble you for a light?
5. It will be a pleasure having the Eliots with us for the weekend.
6. Look out for those falling rocks!
7. For this condition, a patient has a choice of treatments: pills or shots.
8. On long trips, Mr. and Mrs. Crenshaw generally take turns with the driving.
9. Mary Ann apologizes for having kept Mr. Weber waiting.
10. Joseph noticed that the Bartons' children do not generally behave.
11. While Steve very much admired the BMW motorcycle, he told the salesman he could never afford to buy it.
12. The poor village finally received a couple of much needed tractors from the government.
13. Isn't Elizabeth's dress absolutely beautiful.
14. The teacher still can't tell the difference between the twins in her class.
15. Suddenly, one of the overhead light bulbs burned out.
16. The cashier remarked that if her cash register is short at closing time, the difference comes out of her own paycheck.
17. Fred is barely half the age of his 18-year-old brother, Dennis.

Practice Test III

18 In the French-Indian War, the French fought with the American Indians against the British.

19 Sandra sounds to me as if she has a cold.

20 The salesman assured Mr. Ford that there would be no extra charge for the alterations to his suit.

This is the end of Part A.

Now listen to the directions for Part B, as they are read to you.

Part B

Directions: In Part B you will hear fifteen short conversations between two speakers. At the end of each conversation, a third voice will ask a question about what was said. The question will be spoken just one time. After you hear a conversation and the question about it, read the four possible answers and decide which one would be the best answer to the question you have heard. Then, on your answer sheet, find the number of the problem and mark your answer.

Listen to the following example:

You will hear:

WOMAN: What plans have you made for your summer vacation?
MAN: Hiking with friends in the Himalayas. We leave in mid-June and return at the end of August.

QUESTION: How long will the man be gone?

You will read: (A) A month.
(B) 1½ months.
(C) Two months.
(D) 2½ months.

From the conversation, we know that the friends will leave in mid-June and return in late August. The best answer, then, is (D), "2½ months." So you should choose answer (D).

Now let us begin Part B with question number 21.

21 WOMAN: I'm glad you could come today. The drain became stopped up yesterday afternoon.
 MAN: Don't worry. I'll have it open for you in no time.

Tapescript

	QUESTION:	Who is the man?
22	WOMAN:	Here's an ad for an apartment with two bedrooms. It's near the campus and not too high.
	MAN:	What's the number? I'll find out if it's available for immediate occupancy.
	QUESTION:	What are the man and woman doing?
23	MAN:	But why am I being dismissed? There was never any warning.
	WOMAN:	The reasons are several, including frequent unexplained absences and an uncooperative attitude.
	QUESTION:	What has just happened to the man?
24	WOMAN:	Are you paying very much for your apartment?
	MAN:	I can't complain about the rent, which is reasonable, but then utilities aren't included.
	QUESTION:	What did the man say about the cost of his apartment?
25	MAN:	Pardon me. I need some quarters for that pay phone. Can you break a dollar bill?
	WOMAN:	I'm afraid I'm low on quarters myself. I can let you have a couple plus a fifty-cent piece.
	QUESTION:	What did the woman give the man?
26	WOMAN:	First Professor Hart made an excellent case for opposing nuclear power plants.
	MAN:	But in his next lecture, he made those favoring such plants sound just as reasonable.
	QUESTION:	What is probably Professor Hart's own view on this subject?
27	WOMAN:	Now, Mr. Cross, don't hesitate to help yourself to some more potatoes, vegetables or roast beef.
	MAN:	It's been a wonderful dinner, but if I eat another bite, I think I'll burst.
	QUESTION:	What will the man do?
28	WOMAN:	Good morning. Your passport, please. Do you have anything to declare?
	MAN:	Only these two cartons of cigarettes, a bottle of brandy and some silver jewelry. That's all.
	QUESTION:	With whom is the man speaking?
29	MAN:	When I have a day off, I will check our TV set to see

	WOMAN:	what's wrong with it. I would feel much better if you left it alone and let the repair shop look at it.
	QUESTION:	What does the woman mean?
30	WOMAN: MAN:	May I offer you one of my cigarettes? No, thanks. I'm sitting here only because all the seats in the non-smoking section were already occupied.
	QUESTION:	Why did the man turn down the cigarette?
31	WOMAN: MAN:	Your breakdown along the highway late Sunday night must have been rather unpleasant. It could have been much more so. That's when my auto club membership really paid for itself.
	QUESTION:	Who helped the man when his car broke down?
32	WOMAN: MAN:	Professor Dalton caught some students cheating on the final exam and failed them right then and there. Serves them right. I don't sympathize with anyone trying to pass that way.
	QUESTION:	What is the man's attitude toward the professor's action?
33	MAN: WOMAN:	That was really an excellent meal but we ordered far too much. We can't let it go to waste. I will ask the waitress to put the rest in a box for us.
	QUESTION:	What will become of the remaining food?
34	WOMAN: MAN:	Let's see. Twenty-eight sixty plus one eighty-five tax. That comes to thirty forty-five. Cash or check, sir? Cash, but I left my wallet at home. Please keep that for me. I'll be right back.
	QUESTION:	What is the man going to do?
35	MAN: WOMAN:	When did you first discover the window broken and your belongings missing? Right after getting up, around 6:30. That's when I reported the break-in and called the police station.
	QUESTION:	What is the topic of this conversation?

This is the end of Part B.

Now look at the directions for Part C, as they are read to you.

Tapescript

Part C

Directions: In this part of the test, you will hear several short talks and/or conversations. After each talk or conversation, you will be asked some questions. The talks and questions will be spoken just one time. They will not be written out for you, so you will have to listen carefully in order to understand and remember what the speaker says.

When you hear a question, read the four possible answers in your test book and decide which one would be the best answer to the question you have heard. Then, on your answer sheet, find the number of the problem and fill in (blacken) the space that corresponds to the letter of the answer you have chosen.

Listen to this sample talk:

DeWitt Wallace founded the *Reader's Digest* as a pocket-sized, non-fiction magazine intended to inform, enlighten and entertain. He wanted to condense in the *Digest* the best of previously published material. He filled the magazine with articles that celebrated the values he most admired in his nation: hard work, thrift, a calm courage through difficult times, love of God, family and country, and laughter – much laughter.

The first issue in February 1922 had a print order of only 5000 copies. When DeWitt Wallace passed away in June 1981, the *Reader's Digest* had become the world's most widely read magazine, with an estimated 100 million readers each month, and was published in 16 languages.

Now listen to the first question on the sample talk:

You will hear: What kind of articles did Mr. Wallace mainly select for his magazine?

You will read: (A) Those emphasizing the profit motive.
(B) Those reflecting social values he admired.
(C) Those promoting his religious views.
(D) Those written by the best fiction writers.

The best answer to the question, "What kind of articles did Mr. Wallace mainly select for his magazine?" is (B), "Those reflecting social values he admired." Therefore, you should choose answer (B).

Now listen to the second question on the sample talk:

You will hear: What is the speaker's probable purpose in mentioning humor in the *Digest*?

You will read: (A) To stress the magazine's lack of seriousness.
(B) To teach readers many new jokes.
(C) To indicate Mr. Wallace's love of life.
(D) To show that non-fiction is funnier than fiction.

The best answer to the question, "What is the speaker's probable purpose in mentioning humor in the *Digest*?" is (C), "To indicate Mr. Wallace's love of life." Therefore, you should choose answer (C).

Questions 36 through 38 are based on the following conversation.

WOMAN: Pardon me, officer.
MAN: Yes?
WOMAN: We're looking for the big department store around here.
MAN: I'm afraid you're headed in the wrong direction.
WOMAN: But we were told that it was somewhere here in the downtown area.
MAN: Yes, it is, but I meant you're walking the wrong way.
WOMAN: Oh, I see. Could we trouble you for directions to get there?
MAN: It's no trouble. It's only about a 10-minute walk from here.
WOMAN: Oh, is that all?
MAN: Just walk back the same way you came for about a block, then turn right and stay on that street until you come to the next intersection.
WOMAN: That's the corner of Granger and Forest, isn't it?
MAN: That's right. You'll see the big sign on the left side of the street. You can't miss it.
WOMAN: Down a block to Granger and then right another block to Forest. Thanks very much.
MAN: Don't mention it.

36 Who is the woman speaking with?

37 How much farther must the woman go to find the store?

38 What is the man doing for the woman?

Questions 39 through 42 are based on the following short health announcement.

At any given time, millions of people are either thinking about losing weight or are on a diet. One of the most common but least effective means of weight control is the crash diet.

The crash diet is often low in carbohydrates, which are energy-producing foods high in starch or sugar. This kind of diet will produce rapid fluid loss in the first week or so. Many dieters, fooled by the scales, think their fat is "melting off." It isn't. Fat is coming off, slowly, but it is easily regained when the diet is abandoned. And most crash diets, because they are so extreme, are soon abandoned. Also, protein as well as fat can be lost during an extreme diet, and when weight is regained, it is regained first as fat. So, indeed, the crash dieter may end up with more fat than he or she started with.

39 What does a person on a crash diet tend to take in little of?

40 What advice would the speaker give someone considering starting a crash diet?

Tapescript

41 What does the crash dieter lose in large amounts during the first week?

42 After giving up a crash diet, how does a person regain his weight first?

Questions 43 through 46 are based on the following conversation.

MAN: Please come in, Miss Edwards, and close the door behind you.
WOMAN: All right.
MAN: Have a seat over here. How are things going out in the office?
WOMAN: Just fine, Mr. Davis, especially with the recent personnel shifts.
MAN: Yes, I thought so. Well, I and the executive board feel that much of our improved performance in the main office is due to your conscientious efforts.
WOMAN: Oh, thank you, Mr. Davis. My job has certainly become easier since we computerized our record-keeping system. The equipment is a pleasure to use.
MAN: That's true. But we are especially impressed with how your influence contributes to good office relations and improved staff attitude toward the work.
WOMAN: Well, thank you for your confidence. We do have a lot of good people in the office, and the new machinery is wonderful.
MAN: Yes, but machines are only as good as the people who use them. They cannot assure harmony and efficiency in a staff.
WOMAN: That's very true.
MAN: To make a long story short, the board wishes to reward your efforts by making you office manager as of next Monday. That means a $250 raise as of the first of next month.
WOMAN: I'm deeply honored, Mr. Davis. Thank you.

43 How does the woman feel about the recent shift of office employees?

44 How does the executive board consider the woman's performance?

45 What does the woman say has made her job easier?

46 What is the man's main purpose in talking to the woman?

Questions 47 through 50 are based on the following short speech.

It gives me great pleasure today to say a few words in praise of a man we will all miss very much. To be honest, I can't imagine how we will do without him when he's gone.

Bill Masters almost single-handedly built up our sales force in the Houston area and developed the market position that we enjoy today. In only six years, he has brought the firm from a very low fifth position in regional sales to the point where we now outsell all but one of our competitors. Not only have we captured 37 per cent of the market under Bill's leadership; we are increasing our share with each passing month.

As you are all well aware, the company has moved Bill to northern California to work his sales magic in one of this company's most competitive regions. But we know that if anyone can do it, Bill Masters can, and I know you all join me in wishing him the best of luck in his new post.

47 Why is Bill Masters moving from the Houston area?
48 How does the company's regional sales position at present compare with that of six years ago?
49 How does the company now rank in its product lines in the Houston area?
50 Considering Bill Masters' record and the California market, how should his move be regarded?

THIS IS THE END OF THE LISTENING COMPREHENSION PORTION OF THE TEST. LOOK AT THE TIME NOW, BEFORE YOU BEGIN WORK ON SECTION 2. USE *EXACTLY 25 MINUTES* TO WORK ON SECTION 2.

Practice Test IV

Print your name in the box provided at the top of the answer sheet. Print your family name (or surname) first. Then print your first name. You will now have 15 seconds to do this:

[15 second pause]

Now open your book at Practice Test IV and listen to the directions for the Listening Comprehension Section:

Practice Test IV
Section 1
Listening Comprehension

In this section of the test, you will have an opportunity to demonstrate your ability to understand spoken English. There are three parts to this section, with special directions for each part.

Part A

Directions: For each problem in Part A, you will hear a short statement. The statements will be spoken just one time. They will not be written out for you, and you must listen carefully in order to understand what the speaker says.

When you hear a statement, read the four sentences in your test book and

Listening Comprehension

decide which one is closest in meaning to the statement you have heard. Then, on your answer sheet, find the number of the problem and mark your answer.

Listen to the following example:

You will hear: Unlike her brother, Anne usually prefers a small breakfast.

You will read: (A) Anne doesn't like her brother.
(B) Anne usually eats no breakfast.
(C) Anne eats a smaller breakfast than her brother.
(D) Anne's brother eats as much as she does for breakfast.

Sentence (C), "Anne eats a smaller breakfast than her brother," means most nearly the same as the statement: "Unlike her brother, Anne usually prefers a small breakfast." Therefore, you should choose answer (C).

Listen to the next example:

You will hear: Mrs. Weller has on a fortune in jewelry.

You will read: (A) Mrs. Weller owns a lot of expensive jewelry.
(B) Mrs. Weller is wearing a lot of expensive jewelry today.
(C) Mrs. Weller is lucky to be married to such a wealthy man.
(D) Mrs. Weller's family owns the biggest jewelry store in town.

Sentence (B), "Mrs. Weller is wearing a lot of expensive jewelry today," is closest in meaning to the sentence: "Mrs. Weller has on a fortune in jewelry." Therefore, you should choose answer (B).

Now let us begin Part A with question number 1.

1 Jim asked his friend the wisest course of action to follow.

2 Our correspondent in the capital informs us that his report has been heavily censored.

3 Please watch your step as you get off.

4 Mr. Washburn went with his daughter to open up a checking account.

5 The baker offered us free samples of his chocolate cookies.

6 Frank expects to be fined heavily in traffic court.

7 This company's new products have tripled its profits in only one year.

8 The baby has been giving his parents a lot of sleepless nights lately.

9 Mr. Rawlins's wife was pleased that he got her a lovely birthday cake.

10 Uncle Sam emphasized the importance of being thoughtful toward one another.

11 The official giving Amy her driving test told her to head back.
12 Mr. Clinton always goes out of his way to assist his friends.
13 The next bus for the major downtown hotels is due to depart at a quarter to three.
14 Old Professor Higgins is always getting the names of his students mixed up.
15 The principal announced that the attendance figures from most teachers' classes were satisfactory.
16 Everyone can take a seat at that table.
17 Daniel is taller than his mother and nearly the same height as his father.
18 Gary made a loan of $100 to each of his two cousins.
19 Calvin has an excellent chance for a scholarship if his grades are good this semester.
20 There is something about that man's face that strikes me as very familiar.

This is the end of Part A.

Now listen to the directions for Part B, as they are read to you.

Part B

Directions: In Part B you will hear fifteen short conversations between two speakers. At the end of each conversation, a third voice will ask a question about what was said. The question will be spoken just one time. After you hear a conversation and the question about it, read the four possible answers and decide which one would be the best answer to the question you have heard. Then, on your answer sheet, find the number of the problem and mark your answer.

Listen to the following example:

You will hear:

WOMAN: What plans have you made for your summer vacation?
MAN: Hiking with friends in the Himalayas. We leave in mid-June and return at the end of August.

QUESTION: How long will the man be gone?

You will read: (A) A month.
              (B) 1½ months.
              (C) Two months.
              (D) 2½ months.

Tapescript

From the conversation, we know that the friends will leave in mid-June and return in late August. The best answer, therefore, is (D), "2½ months." So you should choose answer (D).

Now let us begin Part B with question number 21.

21	MAN:	I thought you would have the repairman come fix the water heater.
	WOMAN:	I tried calling him all day but his phone apparently was out of order.
	QUESTION:	Why didn't the woman have the repairman come?
22	MAN:	Hello, this is Dr. Muller calling. Is this Mrs. Weiner?
	WOMAN:	No, this is Mrs. Pennington, Mrs. Weiner's sister. Mrs. Weiner isn't in right now. Can I take a message?
	QUESTION:	Who answered the phone?
23	MAN:	This perfume is a present, so I would appreciate having it wrapped.
	WOMAN:	Our gift-wrapping department does that up on the third floor. The charge is quite reasonable.
	QUESTION:	Who does the woman suggest should wrap the present?
24	WOMAN:	My program says intermission is for thirty minutes. So Act II won't begin before 9:00.
	MAN:	Then let's stretch our legs and get some refreshments in the lobby.
	QUESTION:	What does the man suggest they do?
25	WOMAN:	I can't cash your traveller's check without some identification like a driver's license.
	MAN:	Since I have just arrived in the United States, I have only my passport. Will that do?
	QUESTION:	Why does the man offer the woman his passport?
26	MAN:	Dorothy, didn't you get your M.A. before your husband did?
	WOMAN:	That's right. Presently I'm supporting him while he goes for his.
	QUESTION:	What are the woman and her husband currently doing?
27	WOMAN:	How are we going to get home? It's so late the buses and subways have all stopped running.
	MAN:	It looks as though we have no choice but to call a cab.
	QUESTION:	How will the couple get home?

Practice Test IV

28	WOMAN:	How does the X-ray look, Dr. Fleming? You won't have to pull the tooth, I hope.
	MAN:	We can probably save it, but the cavity is quite large.
	QUESTION:	What does Dr. Fleming expect to do with the tooth?
29	WOMAN:	Did Henry tell you whether he would help us prepare this chemistry lab report?
	MAN:	I have dialed his number repeatedly but keep getting a busy signal.
	QUESTION:	Will Henry help the man and woman with the report?
30	WOMAN:	Hi, Mr. Talcott. Is my prescription ready?
	MAN:	It's right here. Just follow these directions and take one pill right after each meal.
	QUESTION:	What's the man's occupation?
31	MAN:	In the old days, people took pride in their work and built things to last.
	WOMAN:	Nowadays you're lucky if they don't fall apart before you get them home.
	QUESTION:	How do the man and woman feel about products manufactured nowadays?
32	MAN:	After his accident, doctors gave Ben little chance of surviving, much less of playing golf professionally again.
	WOMAN:	It's incredible that Ben was back on the golf course again within eighteen months.
	QUESTION:	What is known about Ben eighteen months after the accident?
33	MAN:	Stand back, everyone. This beer was in the car a long time and is a little warm.
	WOMAN:	Well, just point it away from us, if you don't mind.
	QUESTION:	What is the man about to do that concerns the woman?
34	WOMAN:	Well, Jack, I would offer you another drink but I have guests coming and I haven't even begun to prepare the dinner. Thanks for stopping by.
	MAN:	Thanks for the drink. It has been nice seeing you too.
	QUESTION:	Why did the woman mention her dinner guests?
35	MAN:	These air mail envelopes cost 50 cents a dozen.
	WOMAN:	A couple of dozen should certainly do.
	QUESTION:	How many envelopes will the man and woman buy?

Tapescript

This is the end of Part B.

Now look at the directions for Part C, as they are read to you.

Part C

Directions: In this part of the test, you will hear several short talks and/or conversations. After each talk or conversation, you will be asked some questions. The talks and questions will be spoken just one time. They will not be written out for you, so you will have to listen carefully in order to understand and remember what the speaker says.

When you hear a question, read the four possible answers in your test book and decide which one would be the best answer to the question you have heard. Then, on your answer sheet, find the number of the problem and fill in (blacken) the space that corresponds to the letter of the answer you have chosen.

Listen to this sample talk:

DeWitt Wallace founded the *Reader's Digest* as a pocket-sized, non-fiction magazine intended to inform, enlighten and entertain. He wanted to condense in the *Digest* the best of previously published material. He filled the magazine with articles that celebrated the values he most admired in his nation: hard work, thrift, a calm courage through difficult times, love of God, family and country, and laughter – much laughter.

The first issue in February 1922 had a print order of only 5000 copies. When DeWitt Wallace passed away in June 1981, the *Reader's Digest* had become the world's most widely read magazine, with an estimated 100 million readers each month, and was published in 16 languages.

Now listen to the first question on the sample talk:

You will hear: What kind of articles did Mr. Wallace mainly select for his magazine?

You will read: (A) Those emphasizing the profit motive.
      (B) Those reflecting social values he admired.
      (C) Those promoting his religious views.
      (D) Those written by the best fiction writers.

The best answer to the question, "What kind of articles did Mr. Wallace mainly select for his magazine?" is (B), "Those reflecting social values he admired." Therefore, you should choose answer (B).

Now listen to the second question on the sample talk:

You will hear: What is the speaker's probable purpose in mentioning humor in the *Digest*?

You will read: (A) To stress the magazine's lack of seriousness.
      (B) To teach readers many new jokes.

Practice Test IV

    (C) To indicate Mr. Wallace's love of life.
    (D) To show that non-fiction is funnier than fiction.

The best answer to the question, "What is the speaker's probable purpose in mentioning humor in the *Digest*?" is (C), "To indicate Mr. Wallace's love of life." Therefore, you should choose answer (C).

Questions 36 through 38 are based on the following short conversation.

WOMAN:	May I help you?
MAN:	Yes, I would like some tickets for next week's performance of the Bolshoi Ballet.
WOMAN:	Which performance do you wish to attend? There will be three, Thursday and Friday evenings and then a matinee on Sunday.
MAN:	Are there still seats available for all three performances?
WOMAN:	Not many, and very few together. How many tickets do you want?
MAN:	Just two, preferably together. The date is less important.
WOMAN:	I have two together in the last row of the balcony for Sunday's matinee.
MAN:	That would be fine. How much are they?
WOMAN:	$10 each. That will be $20 for the two tickets.
MAN:	Yes, here you are. Thank you.
WOMAN:	You're very welcome.

36 When will the ballet performances take place?

37 When will the man attend?

38 What is the man's most important consideration in buying the tickets?

Questions 39 through 42 are based on the following telephone conversation.

MAN:	Hello. International Airlines, reservations.
WOMAN:	Hello. I'm calling to reconfirm my flight to London on Monday.
MAN:	Your name, please?
WOMAN:	Lydia Fletcher.
MAN:	One moment, please. (pause) Yes, Mrs. Fletcher, your economy-class seat has been reconfirmed.
WOMAN:	And my connecting flight to Helsinki?
MAN:	According to my monitor, that hasn't yet been confirmed on Air Scandia.
WOMAN:	Oh, why is that? I made these reservations last week.
MAN:	There have been some computer problems the last few days, but these are being cleared up now.
WOMAN:	It's vital that I make that connection. What do you suggest I do?
MAN:	Don't worry, Mrs. Fletcher. I have your telephone number here. As soon as the information comes through, I will personally call you back.

Tapescript

WOMAN: That's very kind of you. Thank you very much.
MAN: It's my pleasure. And thank you for flying International Airlines.

39 What is the purpose of the telephone call?
40 Which of the woman's flights have been reconfirmed?
41 What difficulty with the system does the airline clerk mention?
42 How does the airline clerk promise to help the caller?

Questions 43 through 46 are based on the following lecture.

A number of values and beliefs in traditional societies tend to decrease the amount of money people are willing and able to take from their income and make available for productive investment. In many of these societies, gold and silver, houses and land have been some of the ways in which wealth has been stored. Attempts to encourage people to keep their savings in monetary form often meet strong resistance, which is simply increased in times like these of rapid inflation.

Perhaps the greatest obstacle to increasing savings and investments in the traditional society is the pressure of increasing population. In such countries, there is still a direct relationship between the amount of food available and the number of children who survive. A larger food supply often leads to an immediate increase in the number of people who must be fed and thus cannot be used to increase the standard of living.

43 For productive investment, how must wealth be stored, according to the speaker?
44 How do beliefs and values tend to affect investment in the traditional society?
45 What does inflation tend to increase in the traditional society?
46 According to the speaker, what is the greatest obstacle to productive investment in such societies?

Questions 47 through 50 are based on the following conversation.

WOMAN: Hi, Ray
MAN: Oh, hi, Diane.
WOMAN: I'm sorry to bother you at supper time.
MAN: Oh, it's no bother. We just finished eating. Won't you come in?
WOMAN: I can't. Our little girl Emily has come down with a high fever.
MAN: I'm sorry. Is it serious?
WOMAN: I'm not sure yet. We're taking her to the clinic in a little while.
MAN: Is there anything I can do to help?
WOMAN: I appreciate your asking. That's why I'm here.
MAN: What can we do for you?
WOMAN: While we're at the clinic with Emily, would you mind keeping

Practice Test IV

	an eye on the baby? We can't take him along.
MAN:	Be happy to. Is he sleeping?
WOMAN:	Yes, he fell asleep right after his feeding. And his diapers have just been changed.
MAN:	Margie can go over to your place and stay with him, while I finish up the dishes for her.
WOMAN:	We really appreciate your helping us out like this. Sorry for the inconvenience.
MAN:	Not at all. Isn't that what neighbors are for?

47 Why is the woman at the man's door?

48 What will the woman do shortly?

49 What is the woman's baby doing now?

50 At the end of the conversation, how does the man feel?

THIS IS THE END OF THE LISTENING COMPREHENSION PORTION OF THE TEST. LOOK AT THE TIME NOW, BEFORE YOU BEGIN WORK ON SECTION 2. USE *EXACTLY 25 MINUTES* TO WORK ON SECTION 2.

Answer Key

Practice Test I

Section 1
Listening Comprehension

1 B	5 A	9 A	13 C	17 B
2 C	6 D	10 A	14 B	18 D
3 B	7 C	11 D	15 D	19 B
4 C	8 A	12 D	16 B	20 A
21 A	24 D	27 C	30 B	33 D
22 B	25 C	28 A	31 A	34 C
23 C	26 B	29 D	32 C	35 A
36 D	39 B	42 B	45 D	48 A
37 B	40 D	43 A	46 B	49 D
38 A	41 C	44 C	47 B	50 C

Section 2
Structure and Written Expression

Part A

1. C This is the habitual past, requiring *used to* plus the infinitive form of a verb.
2. A The subordinate clause takes the subjunctive after the adjective "essential," so the base form of the verb *reduce* is used (for all persons).
3. B The subject of the main clause must be the same as the understood subject of the introductory present perfect participial phrase (*we*). Understood: "*We* had arrived ... barely in time, and we reached our seats ..."
4. D The introductory conditional clause requires either *Unless* or: "*If* the rhinoceros is *not* carefully protected, ..."
5. D The noun "food" is uncountable so the quantifier *a little* is used instead of *a few*. *A little* is used to provide positive emphasis after the first clause emphasizing consumption of most of the food. *Little* would be wrong because it has negative (i.e., the opposite) emphasis.
6. C The preposition *by* plus the gerund answer the question of how – of the way, or of the means by which – something is done.
7. A The infinitive phrase has been reduced from: "... a large sandbox which they could play in," to: "... a large sandbox *to play in*."
8. B When "day" is modified by an adjective, the preposition *on* is required; e.g., "on a cold day," "on an extraordinarily beautiful day."
9. A "By the end" is already in the past, and "most people" had already departed before that time, so the past perfect tense is indicated.

Key

10 C Since there are only two shoes, the one remaining requires the definite article in reference to "the other shoe (that we know) the boy was wearing."
11 C The words *the wrong* go together, preceding the noun or pronoun. There is no logical reason to explain why the definite article is used, since the noun following is most likely *not* familiar to both speakers in the exchange.
12 A The verb *go* is followed by an adjective, and the phrase often has a strongly negative connotation; e.g., "go crazy," "go bankrupt," "go berserk," etc.
13 B After the causative verb *have*, two forms are possible: (1) the active voice infinitive (without *to*): ". . . of having (someone) blow his store up . . ."; or (2) the passive voice: ". . . of having his store blown up (by someone) . . ." Here, the second form is needed as we do not know who did the action.
14 B This present tense sentence is introduced by a negative phrase, "hardly ever," requiring the auxiliary verb *do* transposed before the subject, *people*.
15 D "Corn" is an uncountable noun here, calling for the pronoun referent *it*. Idiomatically, the word "quite" can modify the phrase *a lot of* but not the word *much*.

Part B

16 A In speech, the word "have" in the correct verb phrase, *could have won*, is actually pronounced like the weak form of "of," because the *h* is dropped and the unstressed vowel becomes a schwa.
17 B "Cost" is singular so the verb must be *goes*.
18 B The pronoun refers to the direct object, "his students," so the reflexive pronoun must be *themselves*.
19 A The ordinal number "second" requires a singular noun to follow it.
20 D For good parallel structure, the first "and" here must connect two present participial phrases: ". . . attending concerts and *seeing* Hollywood and Disneyland."
21 B The sentence must read either: (1) *should cross this . . .* or (2) *should go across this . . .*.
22 D Since only two things are compared, the sentence must end with *the higher*.
23 C The noun "result" is countable, and this common expression always reads: . . . *as a result of* . . . .
24 A We "find out" information (something intangible or abstract), but we *find* something (or someone) that is tangible or concrete (i.e., that can be perceived).
25 B This sentence requires the passive construction: "It is commonly *understood* (by people) that . . . ."
26 C The passive verb phrase "is composed" is idiomatically followed by the preposition *of*, not by *by*.
27 D The singular subject "the side" requires the present-tense verb form *wins*.
28 C The verb "makes" here must be followed first by the direct object *it* and second by the adjectival modifier (modifying the direct object) *impossible*. To prevent awkwardness, the semantically empty pronoun *it* replaces the true direct object – the last ten words of the sentence – which is itself transposed to the end of the sentence. Delete *is*.
29 D The given phrase is an adjective (*more*) plus a noun (*cost*). This word order must be reversed, giving the verb *cost* and the pronominal direct object *more*.
30 D The words *those of* have no referent in the sentence. If they are deleted, the sentence is right.
31 C The second "and" in the sentence must connect two (finite) present-tense

Practice Test I

verbs for the (plural) relative-pronoun subject: "... that block arteries and result in great ..."

32 A In English, it is either: (1) *The First World War* or (2) *World War I*. The grammar of these two alternative names (meaning exactly the same thing) can not be mixed.

33 A The word *such* is required before noun phrases followed by *that*. The word *so* is required when it is followed by an adjective and then *that*.

34 C Since the word "need" is followed here by a noun phrase, the preposiiton *for* is required. *To* would be correct only if followed by an infinitive phrase (e.g., "to promote economic development").

35 C The idiom (*be*) *up to* meaning "to depend on" can be modified only by the adverbial phrase *very much*, never by the single adverb *very*.

36 D The English expression "to do (something) for (someone)" has a positive connotation, while the expression "to do (something) to (someone)" usually has a quite negative connotation.

37 D The impersonal pronoun must be plural, like its referent, "positions."

38 A The pronoun *they* is redundant after the compound subject and must be omitted.

39 C In this idiomatic grammar the subject *it* should be dropped after "more than," but the singular verb *was* should be retained.

40 B This is the wrong preposition; *besides* means "in addition to" while *beside* means "next to."

Section 3
Reading Comprehension and Vocabulary

1 A	7 C	13 B	19 A	25 B
2 A	8 B	14 C	20 D	26 D
3 D	9 B	15 D	21 B	27 A
4 A	10 A	16 A	22 D	28 B
5 B	11 C	17 B	23 B	29 C
6 C	12 B	18 C	24 A	30 D

Questions 31–35

31 A By keeping heat from "dissipat(ing) into outer space," the greenhouse effect is assumed to hold it in the earth's atmosphere, thus generally keeping temperatures higher than would otherwise be the case.

32 D (See explanation of 31 above.)

33 B Not all scientists accept it as a fact for the reason given in lines 8–10.

34 B line 8

35 D Lines 10–12 mean that the gradual increase in carbon dioxide in the atmosphere has not produced corresponding increases in the earth's atmospheric temperature.

Questions 36–38

36 C A "law-abiding country" is one in which the people obey their laws.

37 C The word "addiction" in the passage is used metaphorically and here really means "great fondness"; i.e., the people very much enjoy reading such novels.

Key

38 A The people tend to obey their laws but enjoy reading novels about crime. Options (b) and (d) are clearly wrong. The passage does not claim that the people obey their laws <u>because of</u> their reading habits (c).

Questions 39–46

39 C The revolution beginning ("under way") will utilize "smart machines" to provide information affecting all aspects of life.
40 C Mankind is (now) at the start ("the dawn") of this era.
41 A The new developments will change all aspects of life. However, the passage does not claim that work will end, (B), or that tourism will grow, (D). Nor does it say people will be encouraged to play more.
42 B Machines replaced man in many industrial processes. Man did not change physically: (A) and (D), and no mention about coordination between workers and tools is made.
43 D The new revolution will help man to do his work more efficiently, because of improved equipment. It will not physically change the human brain, (A), or improve its ability to function physiologically: (B) and (C).
44 D The magnitude of the benefit to man of both "revolutions" probably will eventually be similar. But no claims of superiority of one over the other or of equality between them is made.
45 A The industrial revolution depended especially on natural resources, to supply the growing industries with raw materials (lines 7–8).
46 C (See lines 8–10.)

Questions 47–48

47 A The buyer is seriously dissatisfied with the product and so wants his or her money refunded.
48 C The manufacturer is asking the customer to give the reason for the dissatisfaction. Option (B) is wrong because the entire label (not product) is also requested.

Questions 49–60

49 A The national government pays for all of the interest on the bank loans that exceeds 9 per cent of the principal. Since bank loans to customers are not generally available at rates below 9 per cent in the United States, options (B) and (D) are not possible.
50 C The banks lend directly to the students (lines 2–3).
51 D Such use has increased 700 per cent in about a ten-year period (lines 4–5).
52 B (line 6)
53 C The "shrinking disposable income" of average families means that money they have left after paying for basic necessities has been steadily decreasing, year by year.
54 C Lines 6–8 claim that increases in the rate of inflation and in the cost of the average college education were about the same over the previous decade.
55 C The passage says that they have tried to avoid denying a college education to poor students unable to pay, themselves. The implication is that they have wanted to continue helping those students academically deserving such assistance.
56 B (See explanation in No. 55 above.)
57 C "Private donations" come voluntarily from private groups or individual

citizens, not from the government (i.e., not from "public" funds).
58 D Over the previous decade the rate of inflation doubled while the size of the college's scholarship fund increased more than five times.
59 B
60 D

Practice Test II

Section 1
Listening Comprehension

1 A	5 B	9 B	13 C	17 D
2 C	6 B	10 A	14 B	18 D
3 D	7 C	11 D	15 D	19 A
4 C	8 C	12 A	16 B	20 A
21 C	24 C	27 D	30 C	33 A
22 A	25 B	28 B	31 C	34 A
23 B	26 B	29 A	32 D	35 D
36 D	39 A	42 D	45 A	48 B
37 A	40 A	43 B	46 C	49 D
38 C	41 C	44 B	47 D	50 B

Section 2
Structure and Written Expression

Part A

1 C In the subordinate clause, the subject of the embedded question comes before the auxiliary verb, *was*. The past continuous is used to emphasize an ongoing activity.
2 B The verb "deny" requires that a gerund follow it rather than an infinitive. The perfect form in the gerund indicates that the second activity mentioned (starting the fire) occurred before the first one.
3 A The finite verb *major* in the embedded statement is used in the subjunctive following the verb "recommend" and is made negative with the preceding word *not*. No auxiliary verb is used in American English.
4 C In this sentence, the real subject of the subordinate clause is "50,000 spectators," so the empty filler word *there* is followed by the verb phrase *might be*.
5 B A subordinating conjunction of concession is required. All other options here are prepositions.
6 D The expression "as a consequence of (something)" is commonly used to explain a cause, the effect of which is that which follows.

Key

7 A This is an idiomatic expression after "it's time (that)," regularly followed by a subordinate clause in the past tense pointing to behavior likely to occur in the immediate future.

8 C None of the other time adverbs here can grammatically fit into the sentence immediately after the subject.

9 C The referent for *them* is "experiments," and "carry out" must be separated by the pronoun direct object.

10 D The word *some* here can be used with any noun – singular or plural, countable or uncountable – to refer in particular to a thing or person generally unfamiliar to the user of this language.

11 D The adverb modifies the verb "was known," and can grammatically be placed in four different positions in the first coordinate clause. For the greatest contrast with the statement in the second coordinate clause, the key is most effectively placed at the beginning of the sentence.

12 B The word modifying the noun "text" has to be the name of the subject matter itself. The noun phrase could be rewritten as "a text about economics." Thus, (A) is grammatically wrong.

13 D For parallel structure, the construction: "... both that there ... and that many ..." is required.

14 B The objective form of the pronoun is needed after the preposition "to."

15 A After the idiomatic grammatical expression "had better" (meaning a strong "should"), the infinitive form of a verb, without "to," is required.

Part B

16 A In a non-restrictive relative clause, the relative pronoun can not be *that*. For a person it must be *who(m)* and for a thing, *which*.

17 B Passive voice is needed (i.e., *expected*).

18 C Since there is more than one sister, the pronoun must be plural (i.e., *them*).

19 B The past participle *concerned* is needed.

20 A "In the end" alone is acceptable, but when *end* is further modified, the preposition changes to *at*.

21 C The verbal subject complement following words like "way" and "means" is usually in the infinitive form (i.e., *to pour*).

22 B The word "consider" is followed by a verbal direct object in gerund form (i.e., *passing*).

23 A "Proud" can be followed by both *of* and *that*, but never by both together. Here, the conjunction (*that*) and the noun clause are called for.

24 B The use of two consecutive subordinate conjunctions followed by one subordinate clause is incorrect, so *that* must be deleted.

25 C The sentence requires the reduced subordinate clause "when *necessary*" which comes from: "when it was necessary."

26 D The word "every" is singular in grammar, so the noun it modifies must be countable and singular as well.

27 D The idiomatic grammar required is the distance followed by the word *away* (not *far*).

28 D The subject of the sentence is "reporting" so this uncountable word must be followed by the verb *is*.

29 A The verb "call" is followed by a direct object and then the object complement renaming the direct object, so *was* must be deleted.

30 C There is no noun after "important" to go with *an*, so the article must be deleted.

Practice Test II

31 B When the effect is mentioned first, the preposition must be *on*. When the cause is mentioned first, then the preposition used is *for*.
32 B In reference to one's own body the personal pronoun is used, not the definite article. So, *his* replaces *the*.
33 B The adjective "responsible" is followed by the preposition *for*.
34 D In English, the fixed pairs of words are: "... between ... and ..." and "... from ... to ..." These cannot be mixed.
35 A Here the word *waiting* is required, not *awaiting*. *Wait* is followed by the preposition "for" while *await* is followed by a direct object.
36 D One can be "70 years *old*" or "70 years *of age*," but the grammar of the expressions cannot be mixed.
37 D The referent for the pronoun is plural ("forests") so the pronoun must be *them*.
38 B A transposed infinitive-phrase subject ("... to be safe than to be sorry") is replaced by the empty place-filler pronoun *it*. The word *that* cannot fill this role.
39 C The subordinate clause ("Why ... mathematics") is a singular subject and must be followed by: *is a question*.
40 A The couple felt *pleased* with their purchase. The *-ed* adjective, not the *-ing* adjective, describes the people experiencing the mood.

Section 3
Reading Comprehension and Vocabulary

1 B	7 C	13 A	19 C	25 C
2 C	8 D	14 C	20 C	26 D
3 D	9 B	15 A	21 A	27 C
4 C	10 B	16 B	22 D	28 D
5 A	11 A	17 B	23 B	29 A
6 D	12 A	18 A	24 B	30 D

Questions 31–32

31 B Because the auto industry has improved its technology far more slowly than has the computer science industry, the former has not been able to reduce the price of its products drastically, as has the latter. In other words the computer science industry has improved its technology at a rate many times faster than has the auto industry.
32 C They like to advertise that prices for their products steadily decrease as their technology improves. That is, not only are the products of better quality, but the public receives the additional advantage of ever lower prices.

Questions 33–35

33 B Until now, experts have not been able to be consistent in making their forecasts, so they have lacked confidence in their methods. (lines 1–2)
34 D They have simply looked at past experience and tried to generalize from that in making predictions about the future.
35 B To be safe, they lowered their forecasts after applying statistical methods. They were really indicating their lack of confidence in their own mathematical calculations.

Key

Questions 36–41

36 D No mention is made of fighting wars or operating computers. As for option (C), robots do not direct "electronic brains" but are directed by them.
37 B Since the robots tend to replace workers "in industrial operations," it is safe to assume they are mostly found in modern factories.
38 B Only the shape of arms is mentioned in the passage.
39 D Areas of "peril" are extremely dangerous places. Options (A) and (C) are nowhere referred to. No claim such as that in option (B) is made.
40 D The passage does not say whether the price of robots is increasing or decreasing: (A) and (C). The fact that "the big changeover" has not yet come indicates that robots are still too expensive to replace most human workers.
41 C No mention is made in the passage about where robots are being used: (A) and (B); or what the timetable of introduction might be: (D).

Questions 42–48

42 A The energy was supplied by the water of the Merrimack River.
43 B The textile industry produces cloth and clothing.
44 A When the mills began operating, many of their employees were local farm girls. Option (D) is incorrect because immigrant workers apparently were not employed in large numbers in the early 19th century.
45 C 12 hours per day, 6 days per week is 72 hours.
46 A line 6: Most of the original mills had stopped operating ("had closed") or had shifted operations to the southern states.
47 A Between the 1920s and 1960s, the town's economy became much worse. ("Lowell fell into an economic abyss.")
48 D The town's gradual recovery is said to be "a model" for other similarly suffering "New England mill towns."

Questions 49–52

49 C No mention is made in this advertisement of where the company is located. Option (D) is mentioned in line 1 ("an immediate opening").
50 D The job seems to involve greeting visitors, the job of a receptionist, and answering the telephone ("small switchboard"). No mention is made about secretarial work.
51 D The advertisement asks for "excellent French and English", but only "good German". It can be inferred that "native fluency" is not expected in all three languages.
52 C This is the reason for the request for the "detailed CV," or curriculum vitae of the applicant, detailing his or her educational and work background.

Questions 53–60

53 B The problem is mental, not physical.
54 D The problem afflicts older people, regardless of sex.
55 C Many people are not affected as they age. Statements (A) and (B) are not made in the passage, and (D) is totally incorrect.
56 A Options (B), (C) and (D) are all (mental) symptoms of senility.
57 A A "modest decline in learning ability" is common and is not a sign of the disease. The other three are serious symptoms of the disease, as paragraph 1 explains.
58 D The passage claims that 80–85 per cent of senile patients cannot be cured. It

147

gives no figures on the percentage of the population expected to become senile, referred to in options (A) and (B).
59 D
60 B

Practice Test III

Section 1
Listening Comprehension

1 A	5 B	9 D	13 A	17 B
2 B	6 B	10 A	14 A	18 C
3 D	7 D	11 D	15 D	19 A
4 B	8 C	12 C	16 C	20 B
21 B	24 C	27 C	30 D	33 D
22 C	25 B	28 D	31 A	34 B
23 A	26 D	29 C	32 A	35 A
36 C	39 D	42 A	45 D	48 D
37 B	40 A	43 B	46 A	49 B
38 B	41 C	44 A	47 D	50 C

Section 2
Structure and Written Expression

Part A

1 A In subordinate clauses, the conjunction is followed by the noun or noun-phrase subject and then the verb or verb phrase.
2 C After the verb "prohibit," the preposition *from* plus a gerund is required.
3 C In a sentence with "reason" as the subject, the following subordinate noun-clause complement is introduced by the conjunction *that*.
4 C The superlative form is used to compare more than two persons, concepts or things.
5 D In English, a building *stands* on its plot of land.
6 B For parallel grammar, each half of the sentence begins with: "The (comparative) [that] ...,"
7 B For parallel grammar among these adjectives, the word *political* is required.
8 D A store is "opened" (verb) in a brief moment when it is unlocked, after which it stays *open* (adjective) until it closes.
9 D The emphatic order *right now* is used (idiomatic).
10 A The predicative adjective "eager" requires an infinitive phrase to follow.
11 B The adverb *alone* (meaning "by oneself") is called for. It has no connotation of sadness.
12 B In this subjunctive grammar referring to the future, the word *be* is required for all persons.

Key

13 C The past participle *lost* is used. It comes from: "Many items which are lost are turned in . . ."
14 A The auxiliary verb *to be to* often carries the meaning "to be expected to."
15 A This idiomatic grammar calls for the preposition *by* plus the singular form of the following noun, without an intervening article.

Part B

16 A A relative pronoun, *who* or *that*, is needed between "boy" and "scored."
17 A Because of "tomorrow morning," referring to a specific time, *likes* must be changed to *would like* (meaning "wants").
18 D The preposition must be either *despite* or *in spite of*. The two forms cannot be mixed.
19 C The use of *too* here has a negative and a nonsensical meaning. It must be replacd by *very*. Alternatively, it could read: ". . . as long as a lot of people . . . ."
20 A One can say *Most of* or *Almost all of*. The word "almost" is never a pronominal form.
21 D Active and passive forms are mixed up here. The verb phrase must be *could avoid*.
22 A The word "police" in English is plural, like "people" and "cattle."
23 D The phrase *go downtown* is idiomatic English. Use of *to* in between the words is grammatically wrong.
24 D The word *the* must be deleted. *In back of* is a three-word preposition meaning the same as the one word "behind." In the phrase, "in the back of (something)," the word "back" becomes a noun. The given sentence is wrong because it means the bus is inside of the car, behind the driver.
25 D Because "pieces" is plural, the verb following it must be *were*.
26 B Since *frightened* is an adjective, the word *be* must be inserted after *will*.
27 C The subject pronoun *he* must be changed to *him* after the preposition *to*.
28 A There is no main clause in this sentence, so *that* must be deleted and a comma inserted after "know."
29 B The double comparative form is wrong. The word *more* must be deleted.
30 D *Very much* must be *very many* or *a lot*, in reference to the plural countable noun "copies."
31 C With the negative introduction to the sentence, the words *there* and *are* must be reversed.
32 C In reference to people, only the negative expressions *nobody else* or *no one else* are acceptable.
33 C To create parallel grammar on both sides of the coordinate conjunction "or," the words *it has* should be deleted. (If these words are retained, then the word "either" must be moved in front of the words "the government").
34 A To *go abroad* is idiomatic, so the word *to* must be deleted.
35 B Idiomatically, the words *for example* are used, regardless of how many examples actually follow.
36 C For parallel grammar on both sides of "as well as," the sentence requires ". . . will fix . . . as well as (*will*) *paint* . . ."
37 D The word *back* after "return" is redundant, so incorrect. *Back* must be deleted.
38 D The present participle after a verb of perception (plus direct object) is required here to emphasize both the dynamic quality of the action and the ongoing process or activity.
39 C The word *large* is redundant, and stylistically incorrect.
40 A Without "and" to connect the two thoughts, the present participle *claiming* is required here.

Practice Test III

Section 3
Reading Comprehension and Vocabulary

1 A	7 D	13 C	19 B	25 A
2 A	8 D	14 A	20 C	26 D
3 A	9 A	15 D	21 B	27 D
4 C	10 C	16 C	22 C	28 B
5 B	11 C	17 B	23 D	29 B
6 A	12 B	18 C	24 D	30 A

Questions 31–33

31 D Owners of newspapers want to try out new technology, despite its expense. They are not competing with each other to spend money, however. And no mention is made about their workers.

32 C The phrase "tipping the balance" here means having the greatest influence in helping the owners decide to spend the money. No reference is found in the passage to strikes, managerial upset, or changes in newspaper sales.

33 D The publishers must worry about the negative effect on their business operations of increasing costs – (A) and (B) – and of losing business to radio and especially TV (C). "Their adventurous spirit," however, is a positive element – a reflection of their optimism – not a worry to them.

Questions 34–39

34 B A "rare" problem is one that might occur but seldom does. In humans, the problem is very common.
35 D A problem that is "epidemic" is extremely widespread, even out of control.
36 B The acid attacks the enamel.
37 C The bacterium changes the sugar into an acid.
38 D The acid dissolves the enamel.
39 A "Agonizing pain" is so great that it cannot be tolerated but must be stopped as soon as possible.

Questions 40–43

40 B The traditional notion of a person's being truly educated is related not to the level of his personal income but to the quality of his mind.
41 D The humanities include study of languages and literature but not practical applied science.
42 B (lines 7–8)
43 B They want to be more sure to develop a professional ability needed on "the job market" than to develop a philosophy of life (which includes a personal moral code). Knowledge of foreign languages and appreciation for great art are in general not related to finding a well-paying job.

Questions 44–49

44 B The form simplifies communications between the magazine and its subscribers. They do not have to write a letter.
45 A People ending their subscriptions (C) or buying the magazine at the newsstand (D) have no reason to write to the publisher. For those arranging new subscriptions, no such label from the magazine yet exists.

Key

46 C   The magazine needs to have at least a month's (about four weeks') notice to send the copies to a subscriber's new address after he or she moves.
47 C   Obviously a month's notice will help the magazine avoid interrupting its service to the subscriber.
48 D   Sentence 3 of the paragraph asks the subscriber to "print (your) new address below."
49 C   Boxes 1 and 4: the subscription would be a new one, including no payment yet, since you would be inserting "only this form" into your envelope.

Questions 50–60

50 D   The passage says nothing about the state's earnings from sugar.
51 D   The former waste product has become economically valuable.
52 B   The "oil shocks of the early 1970s" were that because of the drastic price increases.
53 C   Pellets are small hard round objects.
54 A   line 9
55 B   lines 10–11
56 D   The sugar growers now do not need to buy any electricity from the utilities; instead, they sell surplus power to the state's utilities (lines 11–14).
57 D   A utility is a government-supervised company that usually has a monopoly in supplying a basic need to an area; e.g. an electricity-generating company or a telephone company.
58 D
59 A
60 C

Practice Test IV

Section 1
Listening Comprehension

1 B	5 B	9 B	13 A	17 D
2 C	6 D	10 C	14 D	18 A
3 A	7 D	11 B	15 A	19 D
4 B	8 C	12 C	16 A	20 C
21 A	24 A	27 B	30 D	33 B
22 D	25 A	28 C	31 B	34 B
23 D	26 C	29 C	32 C	35 D
36 D	39 C	42 A	45 D	48 B
37 D	40 C	43 A	46 B	49 B
38 C	41 B	44 D	47 C	50 A

Practice Test IV

Section 2
Structure and Written Expression

Part A

1. C The understood doer of the first idea must be the same as of the second. So the subject of the main clause must be *the doctor*.
2. A The verb "avoid" requires an object, when a verbal form, which is a gerund. The form *drinking* is used in reference to present and future time.
3. C The words "or not" at the end of the sentence require the answer here to be *whether*.
4. C The kilometer is *shorter than* the mile. The kilometer is *not as long* as the mile. The kilometer is *a shorter length* than the mile.
5. A This sentence employs the imperative form. The subject ("you") is understood.
6. B This sentence requires a modal auxiliary signifying meaning expressed in the past in reference to the future.
7. C Idiomatically, noun complement phrases containing "the first" are regularly followed by the infinitive verbal form.
8. A The same idea can be correctly expressed as 1) *on your right*; 2) to your right; 3) on the right; and 4) to the right.
9. B The word *though* expresses a reservation, indicating an idea not expected in light of the previous statement.
10. B (A), (C) and (D) all are commonly used in reference to specific series of things. The time phrase *at first* simply contrasts initial events with later ones.
11. A *Go* plus an adjective generally refers to events with a strongly negative connotation.
12. B A direct object (*him*) comes after the verb "call". The second noun here, *George*, is an object complement to the direct object, which it renames.
13. D The first clause here is a subordinate conditional clause. It is in the past perfect form because the hearing of the news would have to precede the visiting of the family. This clause: "*Had we heard* about the tragedy, . . ." comes from: "If we had heard about the tragedy, . . ."
14. D Necessity or compulsion in the past passive voice is required here.
15. D *May* here refers only to the issue of permission to do something, or the absence thereof.

Part B

16. C The noun form *influence* is required here.
17. C The subject complement after "look" must be an adjective (*beautiful*).
18. C The repeated direct object (*them*) must be deleted. The word "which" is already functioning as the direct object of "see."
19. B English never uses *can* and *be able* together in the same verb phrase.
20. A The two events are simultaneous, so the first verb phrase must be "*was being readied.*"
21. B The verb "describe" in English is never followed by a noun clause, but rather by the preposition *as*. Therefore, *that it is* is transformed into *as* (*being*).
22. D The subject complement after "tastes" must be an adjective (*fresh*).
23. A The pronoun refers to "bears" so *its* must be replaced by *their*.
24. C The direct-object verbal form after "avoid" is the gerund (*using*).
25. A General references to materials require indefinite grammar, so here *The* must be deleted.

Key

26 C A subordinate conjunction is required here: *though*, *although* or *even though*.
27 C A clause connector of concession or reservation such as *however* is needed to link the two ideas. *Therefore* is a connector indicating result.
28 A With numbers, the form *per cent* is required.
29 B The subject of the sentence is plural, so the verb must be *were*.
30 B Intensifier modifiers for verbs are usually *very much* and, for adjectives, *very*. The phrase should read *very tired*.
31 D A definite relative pronoun is required here in this restrictive relative clause: either *who* or *that*.
32 D The referent *there* is required to refer to the "islands." The preposition *in* should be deleted.
33 B In English, passengers *get on* large conveyances – ships, jetliners, trains – and *get in* smaller ones – cars, rowboats, taxis, elevators.
34 D The abstract noun *prediction* should be replaced by the gerund *predicting*.
35 D The adverb *carefully* is needed to modify the verb "cross".
36 A The expression in English is "to look forward *to*" events.
37 C The conditional phrase *or else* gives the wrong emphasis and must be deleted.
38 B The doctor's intended advice is to ask them "to stop *smoking*." The given sentence gives the opposite meaning.
39 D The superlative adjective *healthiest* must be replaced by *healthy* to make the comparative form *more healthy*.
40 B The plural form *these* (not *this*) must go with the noun "decades."

Section 3
Reading Comprehension and Vocabulary

1 B	7 D	13 B	19 A	25 B
2 C	8 B	14 C	20 B	26 D
3 B	9 D	15 A	21 A	27 C
4 D	10 A	16 C	22 A	28 C
5 B	11 C	17 A	23 A	29 D
6 C	12 B	18 A	24 A	30 D

Questions 31–33

31 B The entire paragraph explains the development and consequences of electrical instability within a thunderstorm. None of the other three options is really explained.
32 C The changes in electrical charges occur with the collision between the hailstones and tiny ice crystals (lines 2–3).
33 A The stones fall because they are heavy. The tiny (light) crystals are carried up by air currents.

Questions 34–39

34 D The ship was in this area "on a rescue mission."
35 D "The 21 crewmen aboard" here is understood to mean "all of the (21) crewmen aboard."
36 A (lines 9–10)
37 D The information is very valuable to these scientists, although not to the general public.

Practice Test IV

38 D The severe cold has kept the ship and materials on it in excellent condition. Deterioration was therefore greatly slowed.
39 C (lines 15–16)

Questions 40–43

40 D The note suggests the danger of serious injury for not observing these directions, although the danger is not made clear.
41 B The main danger comes from letting the container become too hot.
42 A Apparently even direct sunlight can result in enough heat to present a threat to users.
43 A Since the contents of the container are under pressure, it can be assumed that the effect of heat, which would result in expansion of the contents, would be to make the container explode.

Questions 44–48

44 B The messages are sent electronically at the speed of light, not in printed form, on a laser beam or at the speed of sound.
45 A The laser reads the original message on the printed page.
46 A The laser must "read" the printed image before "translating" it into electronic form, after which the message can be sent.
47 C After decoding, the message must be printed on a new page of paper.
48 B No information is provided in the passage about the cost, novelty or accuracy of the system.

Questions 49–53

49 C The expression "wiped off the surface of the earth" here means "killed" or "destroyed."
50 A It is claimed that "a meteor did the job" – i.e., was responsible for the total destruction of those species which disappeared.
51 D The dark clouds stopped photosynthesis in many plants, killing them. No mention is made of heat, radiation or an earthquake.
52 B Without plants, herbivorous (plant-eating) animals would have starved.
53 C With most sunlight blocked off, temperatures on earth would have become much lower than normal, thus producing "a brief Ice Age."

Questions 54–60

54 C Most new techniques in genetic engineering are intended to modify hereditary mechanisms (lines 2–3) but "others include" options (A), (B) and (D) – lines 4–5.
55 A lines 5–7
56 B They find gene-splicing "the most exciting." (lines 7–8)
57 D He was the first scientist to produce the chemical synthetically (i.e., outside of the human body). (line 10)
58 D He presented an analogy of two totally unrelated circumstances and gave examples of requisite conditions for each.
59 A
60 D

Name

Completely blacken the oval that corresponds to the answer you have chosen. Erase all other marks. This is the correct way to make your answer: Ⓐ Ⓑ ● Ⓓ

SECTION 1

SECTION 2

SECTION 3

Name

Completely blacken the oval that corresponds to the answer you have chosen. Erase all other marks. This is the correct way to make your answer: Ⓐ Ⓑ ● Ⓓ

Name

Completely blacken the oval that corresponds to the answer you have chosen.
Erase all other marks. This is the correct way to make your answer: Ⓐ Ⓑ ● Ⓓ

SECTION 1

1 Ⓐ Ⓑ Ⓒ Ⓓ	11 Ⓐ Ⓑ Ⓒ Ⓓ	21 Ⓐ Ⓑ Ⓒ Ⓓ	41 Ⓐ Ⓑ Ⓒ Ⓓ
2 Ⓐ Ⓑ Ⓒ Ⓓ	12 Ⓐ Ⓑ Ⓒ Ⓓ	22 Ⓐ Ⓑ Ⓒ Ⓓ	42 Ⓐ Ⓑ Ⓒ Ⓓ
3 Ⓐ Ⓑ Ⓒ Ⓓ	13 Ⓐ Ⓑ Ⓒ Ⓓ	23 Ⓐ Ⓑ Ⓒ Ⓓ	43 Ⓐ Ⓑ Ⓒ Ⓓ
4 Ⓐ Ⓑ Ⓒ Ⓓ	14 Ⓐ Ⓑ Ⓒ Ⓓ	24 Ⓐ Ⓑ Ⓒ Ⓓ	44 Ⓐ Ⓑ Ⓒ Ⓓ
5 Ⓐ Ⓑ Ⓒ Ⓓ	15 Ⓐ Ⓑ Ⓒ Ⓓ	25 Ⓐ Ⓑ Ⓒ Ⓓ	45 Ⓐ Ⓑ Ⓒ Ⓓ
6 Ⓐ Ⓑ Ⓒ Ⓓ	16 Ⓐ Ⓑ Ⓒ Ⓓ	26 Ⓐ Ⓑ Ⓒ Ⓓ	46 Ⓐ Ⓑ Ⓒ Ⓓ
7 Ⓐ Ⓑ Ⓒ Ⓓ	17 Ⓐ Ⓑ Ⓒ Ⓓ	27 Ⓐ Ⓑ Ⓒ Ⓓ	47 Ⓐ Ⓑ Ⓒ Ⓓ
8 Ⓐ Ⓑ Ⓒ Ⓓ	18 Ⓐ Ⓑ Ⓒ Ⓓ	28 Ⓐ Ⓑ Ⓒ Ⓓ	48 Ⓐ Ⓑ Ⓒ Ⓓ
9 Ⓐ Ⓑ Ⓒ Ⓓ	19 Ⓐ Ⓑ Ⓒ Ⓓ	29 Ⓐ Ⓑ Ⓒ Ⓓ	49 Ⓐ Ⓑ Ⓒ Ⓓ
10 Ⓐ Ⓑ Ⓒ Ⓓ	20 Ⓐ Ⓑ Ⓒ Ⓓ	30 Ⓐ Ⓑ Ⓒ Ⓓ	50 Ⓐ Ⓑ Ⓒ Ⓓ

SECTION 2

1 Ⓐ Ⓑ Ⓒ Ⓓ	9 Ⓐ Ⓑ Ⓒ Ⓓ	17 Ⓐ Ⓑ Ⓒ Ⓓ	33 Ⓐ Ⓑ Ⓒ Ⓓ
2 Ⓐ Ⓑ Ⓒ Ⓓ	10 Ⓐ Ⓑ Ⓒ Ⓓ	18 Ⓐ Ⓑ Ⓒ Ⓓ	34 Ⓐ Ⓑ Ⓒ Ⓓ
3 Ⓐ Ⓑ Ⓒ Ⓓ	11 Ⓐ Ⓑ Ⓒ Ⓓ	19 Ⓐ Ⓑ Ⓒ Ⓓ	35 Ⓐ Ⓑ Ⓒ Ⓓ
4 Ⓐ Ⓑ Ⓒ Ⓓ	12 Ⓐ Ⓑ Ⓒ Ⓓ	20 Ⓐ Ⓑ Ⓒ Ⓓ	36 Ⓐ Ⓑ Ⓒ Ⓓ
5 Ⓐ Ⓑ Ⓒ Ⓓ	13 Ⓐ Ⓑ Ⓒ Ⓓ	21 Ⓐ Ⓑ Ⓒ Ⓓ	37 Ⓐ Ⓑ Ⓒ Ⓓ
6 Ⓐ Ⓑ Ⓒ Ⓓ	14 Ⓐ Ⓑ Ⓒ Ⓓ	22 Ⓐ Ⓑ Ⓒ Ⓓ	38 Ⓐ Ⓑ Ⓒ Ⓓ
7 Ⓐ Ⓑ Ⓒ Ⓓ	15 Ⓐ Ⓑ Ⓒ Ⓓ	23 Ⓐ Ⓑ Ⓒ Ⓓ	39 Ⓐ Ⓑ Ⓒ Ⓓ
8 Ⓐ Ⓑ Ⓒ Ⓓ	16 Ⓐ Ⓑ Ⓒ Ⓓ	24 Ⓐ Ⓑ Ⓒ Ⓓ	40 Ⓐ Ⓑ Ⓒ Ⓓ
		25 Ⓐ Ⓑ Ⓒ Ⓓ	
		26 Ⓐ Ⓑ Ⓒ Ⓓ	
		27 Ⓐ Ⓑ Ⓒ Ⓓ	
		28 Ⓐ Ⓑ Ⓒ Ⓓ	
		29 Ⓐ Ⓑ Ⓒ Ⓓ	
		30 Ⓐ Ⓑ Ⓒ Ⓓ	
		31 Ⓐ Ⓑ Ⓒ Ⓓ	
		32 Ⓐ Ⓑ Ⓒ Ⓓ	

SECTION 3

1 Ⓐ Ⓑ Ⓒ Ⓓ	13 Ⓐ Ⓑ Ⓒ Ⓓ	25 Ⓐ Ⓑ Ⓒ Ⓓ	49 Ⓐ Ⓑ Ⓒ Ⓓ
2 Ⓐ Ⓑ Ⓒ Ⓓ	14 Ⓐ Ⓑ Ⓒ Ⓓ	26 Ⓐ Ⓑ Ⓒ Ⓓ	50 Ⓐ Ⓑ Ⓒ Ⓓ
3 Ⓐ Ⓑ Ⓒ Ⓓ	15 Ⓐ Ⓑ Ⓒ Ⓓ	27 Ⓐ Ⓑ Ⓒ Ⓓ	51 Ⓐ Ⓑ Ⓒ Ⓓ
4 Ⓐ Ⓑ Ⓒ Ⓓ	16 Ⓐ Ⓑ Ⓒ Ⓓ	28 Ⓐ Ⓑ Ⓒ Ⓓ	52 Ⓐ Ⓑ Ⓒ Ⓓ
5 Ⓐ Ⓑ Ⓒ Ⓓ	17 Ⓐ Ⓑ Ⓒ Ⓓ	29 Ⓐ Ⓑ Ⓒ Ⓓ	53 Ⓐ Ⓑ Ⓒ Ⓓ
6 Ⓐ Ⓑ Ⓒ Ⓓ	18 Ⓐ Ⓑ Ⓒ Ⓓ	30 Ⓐ Ⓑ Ⓒ Ⓓ	54 Ⓐ Ⓑ Ⓒ Ⓓ
7 Ⓐ Ⓑ Ⓒ Ⓓ	19 Ⓐ Ⓑ Ⓒ Ⓓ	31 Ⓐ Ⓑ Ⓒ Ⓓ	55 Ⓐ Ⓑ Ⓒ Ⓓ
8 Ⓐ Ⓑ Ⓒ Ⓓ	20 Ⓐ Ⓑ Ⓒ Ⓓ	32 Ⓐ Ⓑ Ⓒ Ⓓ	56 Ⓐ Ⓑ Ⓒ Ⓓ
9 Ⓐ Ⓑ Ⓒ Ⓓ	21 Ⓐ Ⓑ Ⓒ Ⓓ	33 Ⓐ Ⓑ Ⓒ Ⓓ	57 Ⓐ Ⓑ Ⓒ Ⓓ
10 Ⓐ Ⓑ Ⓒ Ⓓ	22 Ⓐ Ⓑ Ⓒ Ⓓ	34 Ⓐ Ⓑ Ⓒ Ⓓ	58 Ⓐ Ⓑ Ⓒ Ⓓ
11 Ⓐ Ⓑ Ⓒ Ⓓ	23 Ⓐ Ⓑ Ⓒ Ⓓ	35 Ⓐ Ⓑ Ⓒ Ⓓ	59 Ⓐ Ⓑ Ⓒ Ⓓ
12 Ⓐ Ⓑ Ⓒ Ⓓ	24 Ⓐ Ⓑ Ⓒ Ⓓ	36 Ⓐ Ⓑ Ⓒ Ⓓ	60 Ⓐ Ⓑ Ⓒ Ⓓ
		37 Ⓐ Ⓑ Ⓒ Ⓓ	
		38 Ⓐ Ⓑ Ⓒ Ⓓ	
		39 Ⓐ Ⓑ Ⓒ Ⓓ	
		40 Ⓐ Ⓑ Ⓒ Ⓓ	
		41 Ⓐ Ⓑ Ⓒ Ⓓ	
		42 Ⓐ Ⓑ Ⓒ Ⓓ	
		43 Ⓐ Ⓑ Ⓒ Ⓓ	
		44 Ⓐ Ⓑ Ⓒ Ⓓ	
		45 Ⓐ Ⓑ Ⓒ Ⓓ	
		46 Ⓐ Ⓑ Ⓒ Ⓓ	
		47 Ⓐ Ⓑ Ⓒ Ⓓ	
		48 Ⓐ Ⓑ Ⓒ Ⓓ	